EQUALITY AND DEMOCRACY

Also by Philip Green

Cracks in the Pedestal: Ideology and Gender in Hollywood
Retrieving Democracy: In Search of Civil Equality
The Pursuit of Inequality
Deadly Logic: The Theory of Nuclear Deterrence
Democracy (editor)
Routledge Dictionary of Twentieth-Century
Political Thinkers (coeditor)

EQUALITY
AND
DEMOCRACY

A New Press Back-to-Basics Book

PHILIP GREEN

THE NEW PRESS NEW YORK

Green, Philip, 1932–
    Equality and democracy : a New Press back-to-basics book / by
Philip Green.
        p.   cm.
    Includes bibliographical references and index.
    ISBN 1–56584–390–8
    1. Equality.   2. Democracy.   I. Title.
JC575.G76   1999
305–dc21   98–33630
                                                               CIP

PUBLISHED IN THE UNITED STATES BY THE NEW PRESS, NEW YORK
DISTRIBUTED BY W. W. NORTON & COMPANY, INC., NEW YORK

The New Press was established in 1990 as a not-for-profit alternative to the large,
commercial publishing houses currently dominating the book publishing industry.
The New Press operates in the public interest rather than for private gain, and is
committed to publishing, in innovative ways, works of educational, cultural, and
community value that might not normally be commercially viable. The New
Press's editorial offices are located at the City University of New York.

PRINTED IN THE UNITED STATES OF AMERICA

9   8   7   6   5   4   3   2   1

To my students

CONTENTS

EQUALITY AND DEMOCRACY

INTRODUCTION

Setting the Stage

THE PURPOSE OF THIS ESSAY is to explore the multiple meanings of the concept of "equality" at a time and place when the historical ideals and practices suggested by that word seem to be far removed from any concrete and seemingly realizable political agenda. I begin with an assessment of what the ordinary intuitions of most people might be about the division of labor in production (the traditional subject matter of theories of equality), and then consider as well how the sexual division of labor and the social differentiation of peoples according to "race" might complicate those intuitions.[1]

Our abstract intuitions, of course, often have little to do with the concrete life situations in which we find ourselves. The second part of this essay, therefore, focuses on the kinds of institutions and policies that people have sometimes demanded in the name of equality, in order to derive a more usable version of the concept from their struggles. For reasons that will become clear, I call the proximate endpoint of these demands and struggles *strong equal opportunity*, and the kinds of *in*equalities that they attempt to abolish I term *surplus inequality*.

What kinds of major changes it would take to abolish surplus inequality, what the social and individual costs of abolishing it might be, and the potential benefits of its abolition make up the subject matter of the next part of this essay. As

1

a case study, I devote special attention to the egalitarian policies comprehended by the current term "affirmative action"; policies surrounding the issue of affirmative action are especially useful to discuss in that they illustrate the unmistakable linkage between earlier, classically "liberal" versions of equal opportunity, and the more contemporary version that I call strong equal opportunity.

Finally, chapters 7 and 8 ask the questions both why equality does in fact seem to have fallen off the current political agenda and what kinds of supporting beliefs about and practices of social life we would have to commit ourselves to, in order to recover what was once the clearly egalitarian trajectory of modern history. This final discussion turns on the moral notion of egalitarian "solidarity" (a less male-centered version of what the French revolutionaries called *fraternite*); and how some of our existing varieties of group consciousness (especially as summed up in the phrase "identity politics") are or are not compatible with that notion.

Much of the discussion that follows turns on circumstances and practices that are peculiar to the United States. At first glance this is an indefensible procedure. On the other hand, nowhere else in the world is there to be found such a gap, such an immense gap, between the rhetoric of equality on the one hand and the actual substance of inequality on the other. In that unique context the rhetoric and reality in turn illuminate each other, and in their conflict highlight the difficulties we must face in discussing such an elusive and contested concept.

There is thus a preliminary logic to this emphasis on "equality in one nation." Everything that follows, however, finally makes no sense unless at every step of the way we remember that a moral ideal upheld because it is supposedly a universal ideal must in fact be expressed in terms that are truly universal. The discussion of equality therefore properly incorporates an overriding question that rarely gets asked in discussions of that concept: what are the geographical boundaries within which the equality of a people, however it is defined and extended, ought to be demarked? This question is considered at length in the concluding discussion of egalitarian solidarity.

2. Defining Equality

However that or any similar question is answered, though, we must first confront the prior question, necessarily antecedent to them all: what does "equality for us," or for anyone, *mean*? The first thing that must be said in answer to that question is this: Equality should never be taken as a comprehensive description of the human condition. Whatever might be the social state we intend to describe by using that term, even the achievement of gender equality, which would undoubtedly come closest to helping us all realize a balanced social existence, would not at all necessarily mean that we will have achieved the good life; or the greatest possible extent of individual happiness or autonomy; or a wise balance with the natural world; or assurance that individuals will always receive their just desserts; or the recovery of cultural and ethical meaning from the flattening effects of commodification and the technological determination of cultural reproduction; or that we will have succeeded in abolishing alienated labor, sexual conflict, and the frustrating and inescapable complexities of living together in large numbers.

Nor can we even promise that equality, whatever we mean by that, will bring us closer to achieving these other goals rather than removing us even farther from that possibility. Equality is about nothing more than but also nothing less than the particular material relationship of people that has historically been called "social justice." As such the concept has a limited scope; but the life field comprehended within that scope is hardly trivial.

To specify further, the concept of equality has to do with the systematic treatment of representative persons, viewed in the abstract as members (and subjects) of some organized social whole, rather than with the treatment of particular individuals with unique, individual needs and interests. If we simply name some person who we think has been treated unfairly by some social institution ("Mumia Abu Jamal did not receive a fair trial") we are not talking about social justice or equality. If we name the same person as the representative of some socially definable group of persons ("Mumia Abu Jamal did not receive a fair trial because he is a black man"), then we have begun to talk about the concept of equality; many discussions of equality or inequality begin with exactly some such personally compelling narrative. But the conversation only reaches its appropriate theoretical starting point when we leave the personal for the general, as in "the treatment of black men in American society constitutes a massive injustice." (Note that this sentence would still be true, and complete, even were Mumia Abu Jamal to be released from death row and confinement by the time these words are published). "Similar treatment for all who find themselves in relevantly similar circumstances" is therefore the general definition of social justice as equality; how to fill in the immense silences that those vague phrases generate is our problem.

Since the definitions of "similar treatment" and "relevantly similar circumstances" cannot be found in some natural dictionary, but are only created by human beings struggling with each other, the idea of "equality" necessarily has many potential meanings, some of which will even be mutually contradictory. Interestingly, in the contemporary world its most rigorous definition, that of the communal life in which there is no division of labor and no differential reward, is largely the product of its antagonists, who imagine a society of equals as the society of an anthill; of workers and farmers all in blue shirts ("the blue ants"), and an androgynous population in which the sexes are indistinguishable. Few people who use the word approvingly or who actually consider themselves egalitarians mean anything like this when using the word.

What might we mean, then, when we say that there ought to be "equality," or that we should move "toward equality," or that there should be "more equality"? Starting from a well-known classical definition that, typically, is both clear in its implications and yet vague in its precise demands, I propose to arrive at one (but only one) particular version of equality; a version that is logically coherent, ethically defensible, and politically useful.

"With regard to equality," wrote Jean-Jacques Rousseau, "this word must not be understood to mean that degrees of power and wealth should be exactly the same, but rather that with regard to power, it should be incapable of all violence and never exerted except by virtue of status and the laws; and with regard to wealth, no citizen should be so opulent that he can buy another, and none so poor that he is constrained to sell himself."[2]

The utopian community aside, this is, I think, what most of us mean when we use the word "equality." To speak first of power: that a policeman is authorized to arrest me for going through a stop sign, or that a mayor can order policemen to enforce the town's traffic ordinances more or less stringently, is a violation neither of my equal rights nor of any moral theory about mutual obligations. That the same policeman can arrest me for entering a plant that has been shut down by its owner, while that very owner may himself enter and shut down the plant whenever he wants, is a different matter altogether. This is violence exercised on behalf of one class's power, and it is totally unavailable to any other class. And since "class" is not a legal status in a democracy, the owner cannot be said to exercise that violent power by virtue of his status.

But what of the laws? Do they confer legitimacy on this special power of the class of owners? Yes, they do. We must also be aware, however, that Rousseau defines "the law" as coming into existence only when "the entire people enacts something concerning the entire people."[3] There is no way in which the laws concerning corporate property and its "rights" in any capitalist society, not even the originally democratic United States, admit of this description. Thus even knowing that what they were doing was a "crime," American workers who fought back with dynamite and coercive mass actions against the violent but legalized tyranny of corporate capital in the long period from the 1870s through the New Deal, or who occupied factories during the great auto industry sit-down strikes of the 1930s, believed that they were fighting for their legitimate "equality." They had no sense at all of criminal culpability for what they were doing, whatever the nature of the legislation passed by a Congress that did not then, and still does not, represent them equally.[4]

Similarly with respect to wealth: although the literal "buying" and "selling" of persons may not occur in liberal democracies, that is what in effect is happening when one class of persons is able to hire as its domestic servants the members of another class who themselves have no viable option but to enter that "voluntary" servitude. Or when thousands or millions of women can support themselves in no way except by selling their bodies (or images of their bodies) for the delectation of men. But even more: writing before the dawn of capitalism in France, Rousseau could not have a systematic conception of what Marx would later call "wage slavery," and we have no way of knowing what he would have thought of the "dark Satanic mills" and their successors. But surely his distinction between the opulent who can buy others and the poor who must sell themselves is an early version of Marx's delineation of classes in a capitalist society. The one class possesses means of production and is therefore able to buy the labor power of others. The others possess no means of production of their own and therefore are forced to sell their labor power to whomever will buy it, for a level of wages dependent on the operations of a business cycle before which they stand completely helpless; wages which for many are sometimes even less than the necessary level of subsistence.

Perhaps some of us would want to say that if the possessors came into their possession simply by the superior exercise of their talents, or via a lottery in which everyone participated, then no one can object on grounds of justice to the resulting distribution of productive property. That may well be; however, once again no existing distribution of resources can possibly be so described. In not all but certainly in most cases, capital originally was accumulated in the form of land wrested violently from indigenous inhabitants, or from the labor of slaves, or from monopolies and grants conferred by the state or by the monarch, and so on. As Marx said, it came into the world "dripping from head to foot, from every pore, with blood and dirt."[5] And although it might be an exaggeration to characterize the way male supremacy came into the world in that same manner, it would not in the slightest degree be an exaggeration to describe the process as one of possession and dispossession grounded in the exercise of force and the accumulation of both property and power.

If the process of accumulation of wealth and power is ethically questionable, its results are therefore open to question and, in principle (leaving aside for a while the issue of practical utility), to conscious intervention. However, I obviously have not yet defended the concept of equality itself, but have merely said that something like Rousseau's definition is what an egalitarian ought to mean by it. But why should one be an egalitarian to begin with? What is there to be said on behalf of "equality?"

An obvious way of addressing this question is to forget "equality" for the moment and put the question the other way around. Suppose someone were to say, "To hell with equality. Why are we wasting time discussing this useless concept? Let's just have the kind of inequality we're familiar with, which is a perfectly good thing, and be done with it." To this (not purely imaginary) person, we might want to put the question that is usually put to egalitarians. Why should there be social inequalities? What can justify them, other than their brute existence? We do not justify everything that exists: what is their possible function?

The first thing to remark is that we can't answer those questions, at least not initially, by simply looking around us. We have to abstract ourselves from our own already highly unequal society, for which every answer seems to come with its own built-in limits, and is therefore useless as applied to matters of principle or right. Knowing why the caged bird sings doesn't help us answer the question of whether birds must be in cages. It is for this reason that political philosophers often use as a favorite convention some kind of prepolitical state (a "state of nature") in which everyone is starting from scratch. Ronald Dworkin, for example, posits a newly discovered, uninhabited—and abundant—island; Bruce Ackerman a spaceship landing on an uninhabited planet with an easily exploitable supply of "manna."[6] Most famously, John Rawls posits not a state of nature but what we might call a primal state of fairness, an "original position" in which people coming together to make a constitution reason from behind a "veil of ignorance;" that is, they do not know who they are as individuals (black, white, male, female) nor what their social interests are (rich, poor, worker, owner).[7]

In any of these cases, the point is to try to intuit what kind of initial distribution we would think of as "fair" in the absence of a constraining history of particular distributions that, fair or otherwise, have come to seem inevitable and thus to be generally accepted out of sheer longevity, continuing coercion, or the heavy weight of inertia. Following this convention, let us imagine that a hundred people (but any manageable number will do) arrive at some otherwise uninhabited venue (planet, island, etc.). What do our moral intuitions tell us about the problem of initial distribution? If they are to accumulate capital, in its original form of the development of not-yet developed natural resources for the benefit of future generations, and if that capital is not to come into existence as social capital "dripping . . . blood and dirt from every pore," then what would be fair ground rules for its initial exploitation and later elaboration?

One way to begin an answer to that question is to look at what a noted *in*egalitarian has to say about a similar situation (although not at all a "state of nature"). Following an example in which four Robinson Crusoes are marooned on neighboring deserted islands, but only one of them on an island from which a living can be made, Milton Friedman then resorts to an analogy to emphasize the point he wishes to make:

> Suppose you and three friends are walking along the street and you happen to spy and retrieve a $20 bill on the pavement. It would be generous of you, of course, if you were to divide it equally with them, or at least blow them to a drink. But suppose you do not. Would the other three be justified in joining forces and compelling you to share the $20 equally with them? I suspect most readers will be tempted to say no.[8]

What most readers will actually be tempted to say is, "Goodbye!" It is not so much that Friedman's moral intuitions are unacceptable (or nonexistent) but that his moral imagination is so vacuous. He can imagine that these actors are "free to choose" only between either arbitrary "generosity" or a noxious police state. He is unable to imagine what most people will instantly think of as the human (not the "generous") response: to divide up these accidental proceeds so that everyone benefits from them. It isn't that Crusoe One ought to be coerced into helping out the other, hapless castaways; it's that only a very bizarre version of a "human being" would not instantly (perhaps, to be sure, after a brief second of wistful regret) choose to do so.

What kind of rules for living together, then, might free but necessarily cooperating persons institute? Of course they would have to deal with the potential problem of free riding in coming to their initial conclusion—wouldn't anyone who knew he or she was going to be treated as a civic equal find ways to meet only the most minimal expectations of the others? Especially if they came from, say, the United States, they would be intimately familiar with the concept of free riding, in that it is our own—capitalist, inegalitarian—way of life. Everyone who avoids his or her fair share of taxes, makes heavy use of tollfree highways or wilderness areas and then complains about taxes, receives perquisites that other people must ultimately pay for (deductible "business lunches"), is free riding.

However, in a more egalitarian and therefore relatively less competitive society the real pressures would predictably be somewhat different: to perform rather than to slack off, but not to perform too ostentatiously. The more transparent the relationship of labor power expenditure to reward, the more apparent will be *any* deviations from an average expenditure of labor power. As de Tocqueville noted, the tendency among people who conceive of themselves as equals is to conform to an unthreatening social mean: not a prevalence of freeriding (or freeloading) but a general absence of all-out work effort would be the real danger facing our putative society of equals.

On the other hand, in a polity in which fundamental decisions were being made democratically and, again, transparently, the gap between effort and outcome would be visible rather than hidden; citizens would have to confront the meaning of the way they were living. If it turned out that people collectively didn't work hard enough to produce as much of whatever it is they were producing as they desired to consume, then they would become unhappy consumers. It would be their collective free choice either to make each other work harder, or to lower their consumerist sights. It's hard to see how the easily recognizable presence of that choice (which in our society we relentlessly conceal from ourselves by such devices as seemingly costless consumer credit, deficit spending, and so forth) could be said to constitute a systemic defect. Being aware of the problem, they would certainly still want to cross that bridge only if and when they might come to it, and opt for an initial egalitarianism. If they were worldly enough to worry about free riding, they would also know that it's a lot easier to deviate from a general principle of equality, if deviation becomes necessary, than it is to reverse the cumulative and metastasizing effect of serious initial inequalities.

Thus we can most easily imagine that, assuming the problem of free riding to be controllable, they would come to the following conclusion.

Until and unless it becomes clear that an initially equal distribution is unsatisfactory for some generally accepted purpose, all the members of a given social order should receive roughly the same reward for useful services rendered at a similar stage of their lives. People whose condition leaves them incapable of rendering any useful social services (e.g., children, the infirm, the very elderly) should receive the goods and services that their care requires, which of necessity includes the standard reward provided to their caregivers.

What I have done, in other words, is to restate and combine Marx's socialist principle—"from each according to their ability, to each according to their work"—with his communist principle—"from each according to their ability, to each according to their need."

If the discoverers of the New Found Land did indeed, in this way, prepare to opt for what they perceived to be a cooperative, egalitarian social state in which all humans would be treated with equal respect, what counterarguments might be made against their carrying out that decision? In an essay called "The Case Against Equality," one critic of egalitarianism argues, "Inasmuch as people are unequal, it is rational to presume that they ought to be treated unequally—which might mean larger shares for the needy or larger shares for the worthy;" in a book attacking the redistribution of wealth from the rich nations to the poor, another alleges that "it is by no means obvious why it should be unjust that those who produce more should enjoy higher income."[9]

Here we see the three most familiar *moral* arguments against equality: (1) that in a humanly diverse world different people have different, not similar, needs; (2) that reward ought to be distributed according to merit; (3) that people deserve a fair return on what they produce. Let us pursue these arguments to see where they actually lead us.

2) COMPETING PRINCIPLES

Justifiable Inequalities

To BEGIN WITH, we must appreciate that as principles of fairness go, the combined principle of reward according to both work and need is not nearly as stringent as it appears; it is not anything like a principle of sameness, or absolute equality. In fact all sorts of necessary or justified inequalities (as we perceive them) remain compatible with this combined principle. In the first instance Marx himself noted that different people work to different effect:

> . . . one man is superior to another physically or mentally and so supplies more labour in the same time, or can labour for a longer time; and labour, to serve as a measure, must be defined by its duration or intensity, otherwise it ceases to be a standard of measurement.[1]

It is also the case (and also recognized by Marx) that work effort can and must be defined so as to include the specialized training (medical school, engineering school, e.g.) necessary to perform certain socially useful tasks. Thus future doctors would have to earn for training what others were earning for doing remunerative labor. In fact, this is not an inequality at all, but rather the rectification of what would otherwise be an injustice, no different in principle from another compensation equality would demand: the rewarding of parents for engaging in the kind of work known as parenting, insofar as it prevents them from doing other kinds of remunerative labor. In the same way, it would be not an inequality but a rectification of one to give an extra reward to those (doctors, mothers) who for one socially approved reason or another work or have worked what amounts to a "double day" over a significant period of time.

The combined principle, in sum, not only does not fail to recognize but actually insists on the facts of human diversity. It is inegalitarians who would subject all efforts to achieve human satisfaction to an ability to pay money for it; who reduce that diversity to the monolithic single standard of value for money.

There is yet another, potentially much more serious type of inequality which we might also think is compatible with the combined principle. This is the inequality made famous by the philosopher Robert Nozick in his Wilt Chamberlain parable. Suppose, Nozick hypothesized, that every fan on entering the arena where Chamberlain's basketball team was playing (today this might be the Michael Jordan parable) were to put a quarter (deducted from the price of admission) in a box marked "Chamberlain"; would not Wilt deserve this special reward?[2]

Once we tear this parable away from its multiple connections with the entertainment sector of corporate capitalism, a convoluted and biased tax structure, and a rather complete misunderstanding of team sports (all of which together render it ludicrous as a moral guide to contemporary reality), it makes a useful point. There are certain talents or simply states of being—the bodily grace of Michael Jordan or Fred Astaire, the phantasmic beauty of Elizabeth Taylor, the erotic energy of Tina Turner, the uninhibited sexual allure of Rita Hayworth—that can only be fully enjoyed when displayed before multitudes. For that reason, such talents or states of being can't be contained within the framework of reward for services rendered in the form of labor. One automobile is going to be purchased and enjoyed by one person; one Tina Turner concert by a hundred thousand persons, with each one of whom she has at the moment of delivery the same relationship (at least!) as car maker to car buyer. There may be certain forms of fetishism that underlie our collective enjoyment of Jordan, Astaire, Taylor, Hayworth, and Turner, but what Marx calls "the fetishism of commodities," the most decisive lie we tell ourselves about the way we live here and now, is only partially applicable to our relationship with them; for in part we do value them for what they truly are.[3] Here we have a real inequality that seems justified by individual difference in a state of social being; but given the proviso that the rewards can't be passed on to heirs in the form of social privilege, it does not seem to be a serious exception to a general rule of initial equality.

There is a further, potentially even more serious difficulty. Theorists of justice as otherwise different as Ronald Dworkin and Michael Walzer have pointed out that although it might be easy enough to institute a system of equal reward for equal hours of labor, maintaining it over time would probably require fanatical devotion and severe repression. In their absence a black market for labor would almost instantly develop, proliferate uncontrollably, and eventually become the real labor market. Who would hire me to design her clothes when for an under-the-table side payment she could get Oscar de la Renta? Or even hire me to tutor her daughter in political theory when for that same side payment she could get John Rawls? One very instructive exercise in this vein is to think of all the people one knows or has casual acquaintanceship of, or simply meets on the street, and then to ask how many of them engage in purely anonymous, purely quantifiable labor? Excepting places such as perhaps the old Rust Belt cities or the mining towns of West Virginia the answer is surprisingly few.

This analysis suggests, again, that we should hold on to Rousseau's limited version of the egalitarian ideal as well as Marx's elaboration of the socialist principle, because whether it's truly desirable, absolute equality of reward, or probably anything close to it, is not possible (again, outside the commune). As a general social guideline it may be sustainable, but only if everyone understands that it is nothing more than a general guideline, and that the guideline is going to be breached quite seriously. But exactly how seriously? Will the exceptions eat up the rule?

In thinking about that question, we have to appreciate that what seem to be rather minor initial inequalities can become quite substantial over time. For example, if you and I both have the same public old-age insurance plan at current American values, but I have made $10,000 more than you per year, and have invested it in an annuity for forty working years, also at current values, then when we both retire my retirement income will be as much as four to five times yours. This kind of disparity, of course, could not occur in the New Found Land. What the example tells us, however, is that there is a qualitative difference between our kind of society and a simple precapitalist community, and that difference has to be taken into account when applying abstract principles. The complexity, the diversity, and the frantically hypostasized division of labor of the contemporary postindustrial order therefore suggests an amended understanding of Rousseau's principle.

In the example, whereas you would be just getting by, I would have a luxurious old age. On the other hand, not being a giant corporation, I couldn't buy persons or power with

my retirement income; in fact, I could merely obtain somewhat more of the same kinds of goods and services that you
too will be seeking. As to that, what does either of us deserve? We both worked hard for forty years; I was able to
invest more in my future only because my pay was higher
(but considerably less, even, than twice as high over time;
it's the workings of compound interest and the stock market
that have generated the great disparity). Here, then, the real
problem for the defender of inequality is not to justify the
higher amount, for that can easily be done; but to justify the
lower.

In an affluent society, people who work hard for a living
(including those who work hard without remuneration,
such as many women) surely deserve a retirement standard
of living at a moderate level of comfort as well as the kinds
of care that everyone will eventually need. If these requirements are met for both of us via public provision, then the
case for redistribution is plausible, but weak. However, if
your public pension is unsatisfactory on these accounts, the
situation is much different. Then the initial combined principle of equality (reward for work plus the provision of basic
needs) demands a system of taxation that will claw back the
portion of my income (and that of every other income
earner who has "more than enough") needed to finance a
satisfactory level of old-age insurance and care provision.
There will still be a disparity between our standards of living, but it will be somewhat less, and it will be less disturb-
ing. And if the defender of inequality objects that the
principle of desert is being betrayed, we can now reply: I
didn't produce four times as much as my vis-a-vis, I didn't
work four times as hard, I wasn't four times as worthy, I'm
not four times as needy. In the absence of redistribution,

the alleged principle of equality's critics—payment as deserved—is more dishonored than honored.

So the existence of simple material inequalities, although inevitable, is not incompatible with the egalitarian standard, as long as they are kept in check. But this conclusion only leads us to the next, more serious, question. Must a "free labor market," of the kind that seems eventually to be inevitable even after we've landed on some New Found Land, lead to the creation of a social system that is *decisively* not egalitarian, and decisively is *in*egalitarian? That is, must the general rule of equality inevitably be supplanted, as it is among us today, by a general rule of market inequality, with ramifications not just in the material standard of living but in every area of daily life and of social space? In seeking to answer this question, we discover that while inequality may indeed be in the future of a *soi-disant* egalitarian social order, if it includes the kinds of *massive* disparities we've come to take for granted they will *not* be due to the existence of differential individual accomplishments; or of differential "productivity."

No one becomes *wealthy* serving other individuals when those individuals (or families) have similar incomes to begin with. After all, how much of their averagely measured disposable income would a family set aside for marginal increases in the quality of a non-essential good? No one, not even Oscar de la Renta or John Rawls, is going to become unequally rewarded to a significant extent by providing services on an individual basis. Even "Doctor Bypass," whose name is whispered up and down the Eastern seaboard (or on New Planet) wherever particular patients congregate, will earn little extra beyond some pleasant sailing on Long Island Sound, and will have to work awfully hard for that. How many hearts can one man bypass in a normal working day, and how much can he charge the possessors of a merely average income for the privilege of receiving his marginally superior expertise? There will surely be a difference between his standard of living and that of the doctor who spends a lot of time giving antismoking lectures to third-graders or tending the ills of the incarcerated. But it will not amount to very much in the larger picture; will not falsify Rousseau's rule for civic equality; and will not produce negative capabilities for the less well-off (see Ch. 3, note 10).

The fact is that if individuals received nothing extra beyond the special reward they earn by providing special services to other individuals, or producing needed goods for them, we would all be living in an egalitarian paradise (a more affluent version of what Marx called a simple commodity society). There are only two ways in which real wealth can be amassed through the creation and sale of commodities. One, the provision of entertainment to masses of people, we have already discussed and dismissed: it has natural limits (how many idols can be worshipped at once?), and it does not necessarily generate cumulative inequalities. It produces privileged people, but not a privileged class. The standard of living of a Michael (Jackson or Jordan) might be enviable (or enviable and stupid), but by itself it would never produce class envy, let alone serious political influence or power.

Thus in a "free" economy (as opposed to the command economy of a monarch, a nobility, etc.) there is only one way in which wealth with serious political and civic consequences can come into being. It requires, first, the *employment* of large numbers (hundreds or thousands or even hundreds of thousands) of people to manufacture a particular good or offer a particular service, which will then be sold in large quantities (thousands or even millions) to consumers on a commodity market for goods or services. In Harry Braverman's words:

> The tailor who makes a suit on order for a customer creates a useful object in the form of a commodity . . . But the capitalist who hires a roomful of tailors to make suits brings into being a social relation. In this relation, the tailors now create far more than suits; they create themselves as productive workers and their employer as capitalist.[4]

Concomitantly, the kind of wealth we're familiar with in modern times requires for its creation the prior creation by a coercive government ("state") of a legal code, according to which some person or persons (such as Braverman's tailors) is (or are) designated as having an unique and enforceable claim to a portion of the income from all these transactions (to use our favored term, an "owner" or "owners.") Note that our starting point of initial equality reveals that this wealth-generating claim of the capitalist/owner, as in Braverman's story, is *not* a reward for any services rendered or products made available. It is just a claim of "property" right generated and legitimized by a positive law of "property" rights. Some people have joined together in a legislative assembly of some kind and have determined that henceforward "property" shall include a perpetual claim on an organization's earnings by those, and only by those, designated as its legal "owners." Without that legislative determination, nothing they have done would be recognized by most people as worthy of this very peculiar "reward." This kind of "property right" is certainly not an institution found in "Nature" (or in any Word of any God). In short, Thomas Hobbes's argument that outside the law there is no secure ownership but only unstable possession is irrefutable. So too is Max Weber's later assertion that all states are founded on force; so that, by extension, the institution of rightful ownership itself is founded in originally coercive acts.[5]

Nor is the advocate of "the natural right to property" helped very much by adopting John Locke's position in place of Hobbes's. Locke maintained that even where there is no State, there may be conventions that people live by and which secure their property. But for Locke even as for Hobbes, the so-called "right" is still a meaningless word until and unless it is vindicated *by other people*. So are property rights only what "we" think they are? Absolutely; the only point in question is how broadly or narrowly the "we" is to be defined. If I believe that the Chinese, say, should adopt Anglo-Saxon understandings of this "right," I must make a reasoned presentation of my argument to the Chinese. Dogmatic invocations of "nature" or "God," both of which might look very different to them, will not and should not do the job.

Of course we should probably assume that it took a lot of hard work to organize the particular employment-generating institution with which we began this discussion: corporation, factory, law firm, or whatever. But the "natural" or appropriate or "rightful" reward for that hard work is payment for the work done. In the absence of some further argument as to why "earnings" (which are really not earnings at all) should go on being received by the initial organizer long after his actual work has been taken over by other people, we have to conclude that a "free labor market" by itself will not generate the specific, idiosyncratic, and historically determined property rights of ownership; it is eighteenth- and nineteenth-century governments that did that. The "free labor market" might certainly generate, in some cases, a royalty for having invented the good that is being marketed, or the process that manufactures it. This is an inequality that can easily (though not definitively) be defended, as we shall see. Marx's mockery in *Capital* of the feckless capitalist Mr. Moneybags, who asks plaintively "have I not overlooked the spinner?" while the actual overlooker tries to hide a smile, clearly does not apply (at least not initially) to Abraham Darby, Thomas Edison or the Wright Brothers.[6] But even the royalty is still a long way from total control of the manufacturing process *as a coercive social relationship*, with its "rights" of hiring, bullying, and firing.

Moreover, if we begin as we have done, by imagining a society of rough equals, where on earth will the would-be "owner" (capitalist, say) find men and women to work for him on such terms? The problem appears obvious. We know where and how American employers find people to work for them as wage laborers, but our shipload of discoverers does not contain persons who are any more desperate for a job than anyone else around them. Suppose then, one of this group were to say to the others, "I have a good idea. Why don't the rest of you all go to work for me producing the means of our sustenance? I'll take responsibility for organizing the work process, and in return take a uniquely large proportion of all the goods we produce for myself and my family and heirs." We can be pretty certain that without some further explanation as to why this very strange social arrangement should be instituted, ninety-nine voices would instantly shout out, "*Excuse* me?" They would tell him to get a life.

Nor do we need the labor theory of value or a complex argument about exploitation to explain their reaction. Let us return again to our own society for a moment (all these travelers have come from there and are familiar with its mores) and posit the following not atypical situation: A company employs one thousand workers to produce a good, and in a given time period sales of that good return a million dollars in revenue. Those revenues are divided (these figures are not far out of line) seven tenths to the workers; half of the remainder to depreciation allowances, returns on loans, and direct reinvestment; and the remaining half of that (15 percent of the total) to "owners," that is major or minor shareholders, as their personal return on their investment, or profit. Of these, the largest individual shareholder gets one fifth, or 3 percent of the total revenues. During this period, then, each worker will have earned $700; while Mr. Major Shareholder will have appropriated $30,000 in profit, or almost forty-three times as much as any worker.

Now it is quite probable that in our own society anyone in the position of owner will have at some earlier time advanced forty-three times as much to the firm as any worker, since the latter will never have been in a position to advance anything at all. This is not literally true: as Engels remarked, each week wage workers work for free, advancing the firm their entire payroll at no interest. For any individual, though, this is not very much, even were our accounting procedures to be based on fiscal truth rather than fiscal ideology. At any rate it doesn't matter, since all this amendment tells us is what we already knew, that in a capitalist economy capital begets more capital.

So now let us return once more to our uninhabited planet, our Lockean New Found Land, in which no one as yet possesses any "capital" but muscle and brain. Here we are trying to decide, as a matter both of principle and of practice, whether and how a capitalist class shall be allowed to exist and if so, how it should be rewarded for its activities. We soon will discover that our would-be capitalist can't possibly justify a reward significantly greater than anyone else's; not forty-three times as great, nor even much less than that. If everyone else were to sit around playing cards while he worked out a production process (an extraordinarily unlikely hypothesis), they would certainly owe him for the extra time he'd put in; and they might even decide to value his planning capabilities considerably more than their own direct labor efforts (voting him a permanent royalty, perhaps). But the resulting differential would be insignificant by our standards. Again, significant differences of income and wealth only come about when a few people *employ* many others as wage workers (in the sense of "owning" the products of their combined labor). In fact, it's not possible to think that this division of labor would come about "naturally." Or, it's not possible to think that, unless we assume that a very large proportion of people are normally lazy, and only a very very small proportion (about the same proportion, that is, who amass riches) are both energetic and intelligent.

This latter proposition, if anyone wants to support it, is that massive social inequalities merely reflect massively unequal individual endowments. The insuperable dilemma of this position is again that, true or false (and there isn't the faintest empirical evidence that it's true), its proponents can't state it out loud, for reasons Rousseau again spelled out very trenchantly:

> It is useless to ask what is the source of natural inequality because that question is answered by the simple definition of the word. Again, it is still more useless to inquire whether there is any essential connection between the two inequalities; for this would be only asking, in other words, whether those who command are necessarily better than those who obey, and if strength of body or mind, or virtue are always found in particular individuals, in proportion to their power or wealth: a question fit

perhaps to be discussed by slaves in the hearing of their masters, but highly unbecoming to reasonable and free men in search of the truth.[7]

Since we are imagining a society with no slaves, but only free persons, those who secretly revel in their own grand superiority, and disdain the inferiority of large numbers of their comrades, will have to keep their silence.

So Dworkin and Walzer are only half right. Yes, a free labor market will produce inequalities, but it won't by itself produce the kind of gross *division of labor* that multiplies those inequalities exponentially. In the real world's history, no one ever volunteered to be a wage worker. Before wage workers can exist as individuals, there has to be a legally constituted class, or set of social positions, ready to receive them as such. By "legally constituted class" I mean a large group of persons who, first, as determined by the actions of governments have no legal title to means of production; who, second, would be considered thieves if they attempted to work on means of production owned by someone else without that person's permission and under ground rules set by that person; and who, finally, can make no claim on the products of any means of production owned by another, no matter how desperate their own need. In Hegel's prescient words, as "dependence and want increase *ad infinitum* . . . the material to meet these is permanently barred to the needy man because it consists of external objects with the special character of being property, the embodiment of the free will of others, and hence from his point of view *its recalcitrance is absolute.*"[8]

Thus wage workers, as well as those who work without even receiving wages, have to have been forcibly relieved of their options of making a living in some other way, or else they indeed have to be just preternaturally lazy. But not wanting to be a wage worker (or a domestic dependent) is in no way a sign of laziness; it's just a normal, human desire to work for oneself. By far the most likely outcome of our "desert planet" scenario is that the other members of the spaceship colony would say to their putative economic royalist, "That's all right, we'll help you work out the labor process, and we'll vote you an extra yearly reward for your special organizing efforts, but we certainly otherwise expect to be equal partners in making work rules and divvying up the proceeds." At that point the prospects for and justifications of an extreme capitalist division of labor would vanish.

In short, if everyone were making truly equal, truly free choices as to what kind of life to lead, the "working class" whose existence we take for granted, would consist only of all those people who are so loath to be burdened with any responsibility for social reproduction that they would cheerfully trade in their putative equality for the "right" to do nothing but labor at the arbitrary command of others. Needless to say, no such class has ever "chosen" to exist in numbers large enough to sustain what we think of as a productive economy. The people Milton Friedman calls "free to choose" must first be historically *un*free to choose their way of life before they "choose" to be someone else's wage laborer. Only economists or philosophers of the Ivory Tower could suppose that a system of industrial production as we know it could have come into being without massive, armed support from the coercive forces of state, class, and caste.

Marx's discussion of "The So-Called Primitive Accumulation" (see p. 7 above) is still the most authoritative description of how a wage labor class actually gets created. It should be noted that we are not talking about "work discipline" here, but about (in eighteenth-century England, to take just one example), laws of vagabondage and vagrancy that made it a *capital crime* to beg in place of working for wages. It is not possible to read those chapters of *Capital*, or the more densely packed theoretical discussion of the formation of the English working class in Marx's *Grundrisse*, not to mention the later additions of, among others, E. P. Thompson and E. F. Hobsbawm, and then to write such ahistorical invocations of "the free market" as Friedman's *Capitalism and Freedom* or Nozick's *Anarchy, State, and Utopia*. Friedman argued that individuals in a capitalist society "are effectively free to enter or not to enter into any particular exchange," so that "every transaction is strictly voluntary." As C. B. MacPherson elegantly noted in reply, "A moment's thought will show that this is not so. The proviso that is required to make every transaction strictly voluntary is *not* freedom not to enter into any *particular* exchange, but freedom not to enter into any exchange *at all*."[9] And, of course, people who have been deprived of their own land or other means of production don't have that freedom.

Just as the free labor market paradigm therefore cannot explain the creation of a class that "owns" productive industry, it also can't explain the other major component of an inegalitarian social framework that follows in its wake. This is the super-affluent class of those who work specifically for the owners of wealth, as executives, corporate lawyers, managers, brokers, advertisers, all the various manipulators of money and finance, occasionally doctors: those whom Harry Braverman calls the "servants" of capitalism. As I have written elsewhere:

> [The] capitalist begins to imitate the feudal lord with his parasitic retinue. Suppose that instead of a valet, butler, footman,

etc., the capitalist hires a patent lawyer, an industrial spy, an overseas representative, a public relations consultant, an advertising agency, a market analyst; or a personnel director, an industrial psychologist, a floor supervisor, a cost accountant, a labor relations department, an administrative staff to keep a paper record of productive activity; or a tax lawyer, a financial advisor, an investment counsellor."[10]

Some of these occupations might exist in a society of equals in what we today consider a middle-class way of life; who knows? But they wouldn't have incomes much different from the rest of us, if there weren't millionaires, billionaires, and trillionaires to employ them and pay them. These employers pay them, to be precise, not their market wage in the social order, but their market wage within the domain of the super-rich who control most of the assets of that order; and who can therefore afford to pay them a wage that has nothing to do with their talent or skill compared to yours or mine, but instead has to do with their talent or skill from the standpoint of capitalist and corporate wealth.

There are many people with management talent, but only a few with management talent that's been trained to put itself to use within the corporate order. We need only ask whether *the employees* of an enterprise competing with other employee-run enterprises would, if they had their way, pay its executives what Wal-Mart or IBM or General Electric now pays them, to understand again that any "labor market," free or otherwise, is a socially and historically constructed entity. If the gigantic wealth of the corporate world were by general cultural agreement (not coercive taxation) thought to be properly put instead to purposes of social improvement, the excess privilege of its service class (who receive their greatest reward when they fail in their assigned task and are fired) would vanish. Not only would the pool of those who might be considered capable of becoming part of that class be vastly enlarged, but the kinds of persons who today run nonprofit agencies at derisory salaries would suddenly be in great demand. Who gets what and how much they get is nothing more than a product of dominant economic structures and of the kinds of motivations that come to predominate within those structures; it suggests no intrinsic capacity to earn more rather than less.

2. The Question of Merit

Since, therefore, extreme inequality won't come about "naturally," we are led necessarily to the only two truly serious questions about inequality and its justifications. First, is the comparative moral virtue of the *best* among us so overwhelming that we can imagine rewarding their services with dozens or hundreds of times our own average incomes for work performed, in the same way that we might reward Tina Turner or Michael Jordan for their unique services? That is to say, does the *meritocratic ideal* justify significant social inequalities among people who do productive labor for a living? Or, alternatively, are there desirable material gains to be realized from recognizing and rewarding "the best" in a drastically stratified form? That is to say, does *social utility* (usually thought of in this context as economic *"efficiency"*) justify significant social inequalities among people who do productive labor for a living?

As it happens, the meritocratic justification for inequality, divorced from any utilitarian support, can be dispensed with almost instantly; not because it isn't real but because what it justifies looks a lot more like socialism than like capitalism. Any egalitarian, in fact, should be very happy to stand on a platform of pure meritocracy!

We will only fail to appreciate this point if we accept the going notion of "merit" in the United States (and Great Britain as well), according to which "merit" is something that is measured not by performance criteria but by (allegedly) predictive tests, such as IQ or Scholastic Aptitude (SAT) tests. On this understanding, someone with a combined SAT score of, say, 1400, deserves (or "merits") admission to a college at which the average combined score of entrants is 1250 more than does someone with a combined score of 900. (See chapter 6 for a lengthier discussion of "affirmative action.") This confusion is so total, encompassing moral, analytic, and practical blindness, that it is hard to explain. Reading impassioned defenses of "merit" against affirmative action admissions programs, we would never know that Michael Young's savage satire *The Rise of the Meritocracy* was actually a satire.¹¹ It is as though rational choice economists were to take Swift's proposal for dealing with the Irish famine seriously, and start pricing baby meat.

It's clear enough on second thought (if not on first) that a system of entry to professions based on predictive tests is the exact opposite of a meritocracy. Whether quantitative or qualitative, entry tests are nothing more than a rationing device. Even if, in a general way, they "predict" successful performance (whatever that might mean) more than half of the time, this still has nothing to do with any individual. We will only find out if that particular person is worthy of reward for a given type of performance by observing the performance. The only performance written "aptitude" tests can predict with any success is performance on further exercises exactly like themselves. Since no occupation in the world (except that of test-maker) primarily requires turning out aptitude tests, they are virtually worthless.

In Arthur Okun's acerbic phrase, "stress on IQ is a form of

narcissism peculiar to intellectuals, and fortunately has no counterpart in the marketplace."[12] Even in their own terms, tests tell us next to nothing about individual likelihoods. The best (most profound, most original, most interesting) papers in political theory I've read during my years as a teacher of that subject were written by a student with an SAT Verbal score of 495. This fact will only surprise people who are surprised when Route 85 turns out to be so much curvier than that nice little straight line on the map. The map is not the territory, and the test is not an accomplishment.[13]

Merit properly defined, therefore, cannot possibly be thought of as the basis for admission to education or training programs. A real meritocracy rewards real merit: that is, *accomplishment* that benefits other people by bringing out the best in a given field of endeavor, either through hard work and dedication or the exercise of superior skill. A partial judgment of merit might certainly be based on performance during a training or apprenticeship period that genuinely mimics the requirements of the job that will follow; but this begins to be a test of on-the-job performance.

Suppose, now, that our imaginary society, or any social order, were really to attempt to link reward to merit, as the critics of equality suggest it ought to do. Their favorite institution "the free market," can't do the job; as we've seen, those with the most money automatically get to define what's "worthiest," and so on down the line. What alternatives are there?

From the perspective of an initially egalitarian income distribution, it would seem that meritocratic deviations would consist of bonus payments or prizes or nonmonetary honorary rewards to exceptional performers on the one hand, and perhaps the penalty of being asked to find another line of work on the other hand. Or it might be decided that reward should be indexed purely to work effort, as prescribed by a literal (but probably incorrect) interpretation of the socialist principle, without consideration of actual accomplishment and its value to others. Then we might consider the following story.

For many years a gigantic office building in the center of London (Centre Point) stood virtually empty while its owner, a successful real estate speculator, waited to find a single tenant willing to rent the whole building, and meanwhile took a very useful tax loss on his "failure" to get a return on his property. What would have happened had the city, instead, razed the building, and then offered some homeless or low-income families on the one hand, and the corporate inhabitants of a slightly outdated office building on the other, the (now vacant) site, with one proviso: whoever would work at helping to *build* it six days a week, ten hours a day, for five years without vacation, would win the building they had built?

The poor may sometimes *seem* not to work hard, but who has offered them the prerequisites for believing that hard work will pay off in a complex, postindustrial society: that is, the necessary training and guarantee of subsequent employment as an earned reward for successful participation in educational activities or apprenticeships?[14] Can there be any doubt who would have won that prize?

But of course, merit can and very likely would be assessed as consisting of much more than just pure work effort. What about its value to others? For example, differential reward might be based on the testimony of witnesses as to which persons had made a difference in their lives, had helped them fulfill basic needs; and the judgment of co-workers as to which of them had demonstrated noteworthy skill. Or, more practically perhaps, a representative panel of citizens could be chosen to rank the value of occupations rather than persons, which ranking could then be combined with measures of work effort, testimony about individuals, and judgments of skill to create an overall index of "merit." Before the development of input-output analysis and high-speed computers, this procedure might have been impossibly complex, but nowadays the U.S. Bureau of Labor Statistics routinely engages in this kind of exercise, coding occupations, ranking them by mean income, etc. And although bureaucratic inflexibility might create gaps between formal indices and market values, once again a black market for "merit" would develop to realign official codes with expressed social needs.

The result of all such efforts would be broadly similar, although different groups might benefit more or less from different arrangements. Lonely inventors or misunderstood artistic geniuses especially would not benefit in the first instance from definitions of merit based on public recognition, although eventually their royalties might more than compensate for initial neglect. Even more, at first glance an emphasis on public recognition and occupational ranking might seem likely to penalize women performing the tasks of caregiving, including child-rearing and homemaking, since what women do as women is not, in a wage labor—based economy, perceived by many people (or many men at any rate) as "work," hard or otherwise. Caregiving of any kind is for the most part an activity conducted in private. A mother takes care of her children, a home visitor takes care of an invalid, an aide takes care of a mentally retarded person, a woman takes care of her grandmother. Some of these activities are easily forgotten when we think about who produces "value" for society in general; and some of them will even be seen by some people to produce social disutility, if a naive general welfare standard is used to judge them (e.g., taking care of people who are about to die, or who can never be socially productive themselves).[15] Whether from Marx's standpoint or that of a modern welfare economist, such expenditures can be seen as subtractions from produced value rather than additions to it.

To pay for caregiving activities in accordance with the original principle of reward for meritorious effort would require a transfer of assets from those who produce for the public to those who take care of the private. Thus just as does the principle of rewarding the basic needs of old age (to which it is obviously related), the principle that caregiving merits roughly the same reward as any other socially desirable activity implies a redistributive "welfare state," even where rewards for work are distributed much more equally than now (see chapter 3). This does not in principle necessarily mean redistribution from high earners to low earners: that kind of progressive tax system is a response specifically to extreme and entrenched *in*equality. Nonetheless, redistribution between sectors of the economy would *have to* take place without any doubt if the work that women do were to be rewarded for its true value.

It must be kept in mind, though, that in our imaginary New Found Land, half the potential working population would be women, who would be able (as they would be in any consensual social setting, but have not been able in the United States or other contemporary societies) to raise this issue *before* "work" and its compensations were formally defined. Given the opportunity, women would certainly insist on both joint parenting arrangements and appropriate compensation for all forms of caregiving as well as on some kind of welfare/insurance state to meet the inevitable costs of caregiving's necessary shortfalls. And we can be certain that they would consent to participate voluntarily only in a social order that was arranged to meet their particular needs.[16] The "free market," it turns out, not only doesn't distribute the rewards of labor according to merit; it doesn't distribute the rewards of gender according to merit either.[17]

A true meritocracy, in other words, can only reflect a popular consensus as to what constitutes the social virtue of an occupation; and a popular consensus can only lead to legitimate principles of meritocracy when everyone has had an equal chance to be part of it. To say this is not to adopt a philosophically naive position according to which the Good, the True, and the Beautiful are nothing but whatever "the people" say they are. That the Budapest String Quartet won't come close to filling the same venues that are standing room only for Michael Jackson doesn't necessarily mean that his music is more meritorious than theirs; merit and popularity are different categories. However, any discussion of value must at least *begin* with what people actually do value. That is not sufficient to define what is truly valuable, but it is a necessary precondition of any subsequent discussion. The missing element from this discussion, in turn, is not market price nor advertising promotion nor even democratic voting—none of which is designed to produce an approximation of virtue—but rather actual dialogue engaged in by real people about what they think and why they think it. And in this case at least, it's hard to imagine many people concluding, upon such a discussion, that a free market valuation of merit ought to be substituted for one based on a public determination of some kind. If people believed this, the Congressional Medal of Honor, appointments to the Supreme Court, and the Pulitzer Prize would all be for sale. As Michael Walzer notes, there are various goods in life which no one will openly attempt to buy, because it can't reasonably be claimed that they should be for sale.[18]

But does reason perhaps suggest that *monetary* earnings for *material labor* performed for an impersonal labor market should be based strictly on market tests? Again, what seems obvious at first glance is not so obvious upon reasoned consideration. Here, those who justify as "fair" an uninhibited labor market economy in which the rules governing differential reward are not legislated and dollar price alone stands in for value are laboring under a basic confusion. Their confusion is to think that the market really is "a system of effectively proportional representation," which really does distribute "payment in accordance with product."[19] But it is neither producers nor consumers, nor any human beings at all, who are proportionally represented. The rule of this labor market is not one person one vote, let alone one moral sage one vote, but one dollar one vote. (Actually the "free" labor market is a good deal less democratic than that, in that people with incomes below a certain level effectively have no market voice at all, or are even penalized for their lack of purchasing power by, for example, being charged higher prices for similar goods). To make this sleight-of-hand substitution stick, one must believe that in a market society every additional dollar received has been earned by some sort of additional meritorious activity. It may be possible to say this, but it is not possible to believe it. Mr. Major Shareholder, for example, doesn't "produce" every one of "his" products; he doesn't produce any of them. He is being paid in accordance with other people's product.

Nor can this argument be rescued from its visible falsity by positing some principle of "fair transfers," so that any dollar fairly earned may be disposed of—passed on to others—as the original owner wishes, *ad infinitum*.[20] Aside from its historical absurdity (see above), this amendment merely begs the question. Complex rules about appropriation, ownership, inheritance, and so on, except when they are about the most basic elements of moral law, such as the prohibition against theft of another's personal goods, are neither "fair" nor "unfair." As we've seen in discussing "property," they are merely rules. To paraphrase Marx, "natural" resources do not come into the world with laws about their "ownership" stamped on their foreheads.

If I have a piece of land which someone has awarded to me as my "property," and you have an abutting piece of land that is your "property," who "owns" the subsoil rights under my land if a vein of some valued resource that you have exploited under your land turns out to extend under mine? If I explore the wilderness or build a railroad while my wife stays home and cares for our children, why should the resulting accumulation be "mine" rather than "ours" or even "hers"? Some of the world's most immense fortunes have been built up out of the answers to such questions. These answers have had nothing to do with considerations of "fairness" and everything to do with the alleged relationship between the the exploitation of resources, certain kinds of consequent economic growth, and definitions of social utility. In every case, moreover, decisions about the most appropriate way to define that relationship have been made by or on behalf of those who happened to be the most politically and socially powerful persons at the time.

In short, if an American Congress representing a different constellation of power were ever to adopt legislation commanding preference in reward for those who do really essential work, then the aisles at Neiman-Marcus would be thronged by oil-field roustabouts, police officers and firefighters (or their spouses), the directors of nonprofit social service agencies, home care nurses, single mothers who've never practiced birth control, and so on. Moreover, at present the sphere of basic needs provision, located overwhelmingly in "women's work," goes unpaid or underpaid; to pay *everyone* "in accordance with product" would be to overturn totally all existing relationships between men and women.[21] Far from mimicking our contemporary way of life, the transfer of income and wealth brought about by "payment in accordance with product" would shake the foundations of our own or any contemporary society.

3) EQUAL OPPORTUNITY

What Is "Equal Opportunity"?

WHAT THE FOREGOING DISCUSSION MAKES clear is that most of the rules that foster inequality among men and women in societies without traditional, formal hierarchies of caste and class are not based on merit at all but are rather created by powerful persons and then justified by notions of social utility or, as in the case of gender discrimination, by a long history of custom and convention. At this point, then, we should recast our discussion, as follows.

Pure equality of reward is not possible, and most people probably do not think it is desirable. Equality of *opportunity*, rather, is the general social desideratum in most advanced capitalist social orders, and it is the utility of equal opportunity that we should now discuss. This restatement of our real subject matter is still fairly meaningless, however, in that "equality of opportunity" itself, without a good deal of further specification, is a fairly meaningless phrase. In the United States, for instance, most concrete politics (aside from the politics of sectarian fringes) consists of a fierce ideological struggle between hostile partisans of "equal opportunity" whose usages and understandings of the term are wholly opposed. Once, "equal opportunity" was the slogan of the American Left (that is, the New Deal liberal–labor coalition) against the traditionalism of the elitist Right. Since the collapse of the civil rights movement as a force and the realigning election of 1968 that slogan has come to be appropriated by a Right that is no longer overtly hierarchical but is now *soi-disant* populist (what the British sociologist Stuart Hall calls "authoritarian populism"); just as in Britain Margaret Thatcher took over the concept of "opportunity" (without "equal" attached to it) and so for two decades redefined the Tories as the "progressive" and "democratic" party.[1]

The first of these opposed usages, both historically and conceptually, is formal, legal, equal opportunity: what the French in the eighteenth century called "careers open to the talents." Equal opportunity in this understanding has both a positive and a negative component. Positively, "careers open to the talents" means the abolition of institutionalized privilege. There may only be a limited number of positions available for a much greater number of talented people, but at least they will not already have been filled by aristocrats born into them, the sons of their previous holders, and so on. They are there to be filled by anyone. Negatively, formal equal opportunity means nondiscrimination. In principle, no one is to be barred from any of these available positions or career ladders. Anyone who fails in the pursuit of a desired career path may have lost out because of (comparative) lack of talent, lack of the initiative necessary to learn how to use one's talent, or sheer bad luck. These are the only legitimate grounds of unequal accomplishment in an equal opportunity society.

The anomaly of the British Isles aside, the capitalist democracies have achieved equal opportunity in this sense. In the United States, only the preference that elite colleges and universities still give to applicants who are "legacies" remains as a reminder of inherited privilege (which never truly existed in the United States in any event). As for discrimination, though still immense and intense, it mostly remains at the level of tacit or informal (that is, extra-legal) behavior. To be caught with a "smoking gun," as was the Texaco corporation most recently (in that case, a live cassette), is instantly to fall afoul of both the law and public opinion. It isn't that millions of people may not think the way those Texaco executives thought but that there's a generally accepted proscription against conducting public business on such a basis.

To grant this much is only the beginning of a discussion of equal opportunity, however. There are at least two serious difficulties in achieving equal treatment in the formally equal polity. The first is a problem inherent in the idea and institutions of nondiscrimination itself. The gendered and in some nations (especially the United States) the racial structuration of the law is such that equal treatment for men and women necessarily produces unequal outcomes for women; formally equal treatment for blacks and whites (for example) necessarily produces unequal outcomes for blacks. This paradox inheres in any version of equal treatment; it is discussed at length in chapter 6.

Beyond the legal order's potential for self-contradiction is a broader difficulty: the immense gap between legal appearances and social realities in any society marked by extreme differences in wealth and income and extreme variation in what is expected of men and women, or which consists of a dominant social group and minorities. Even after formal legal privilege and discrimination have been abolished, it still remains the case that a large number of people may "fail" in their quest for an ordinarily rewarding life, neither through any fault of their own nor because of bad luck; but rather because serious material and structural obstacles have been systematically put in their way. In this respect the reality of "equal opportunity" is denied, and in practice the ideal becomes a sham.

More precisely, opportunity remains decisively unequal if initial inequalities of condition and circumstance are *cumulative* and *interactive*; and if their cumulative weight is so great as to be beyond the control of any normal (i.e., nonheroic) individual. As Michael Parenti describes some very common American inequalities, for example:

> To be conceived in poverty is to suffer risks while still inside the womb. Insufficient prenatal care, poor diet, and difficult working conditions for lower-class women leave them more likely to produce miscarriages, premature births, mentally and physically damaged infants. Once born, the lower-class child faces conditions of malnutrition, infection, and inadequate health care that may lead to maldevelopment of the central nervous system and mental retardation. Indeed, the poor of *all* age brackets suffer proportionally far more than do those of higher income from tuberculosis, rheumatic fever, food poisoning, epilepsy, polio, diptheria, brucellosis, silicosis, and venereal disease . . .[2]

So, in the 1990s, a young boy growing up in Harlem has less chance of living to age forty than does the average Bangladeshi male. Clearly this condition has nothing to do with "race," "genes," etc. The United States is full of other African American males who have a much better chance of living to age forty than the average Bangladeshi male. What is happening, as Amartya K. Sen points out, is that "being poor in a rich society is itself a capability handicap . . . *Relative* deprivation in the space of *incomes* can yield *absolute* deprivation in the space of *capabilities*. In a country that is generally rich, more money may be needed to buy enough commodities to achieve the *same social functioning*, such as . . . 'taking part in the life of the community.'"[3] Thus, for example, defenders of "the family" against the "welfare state" in the United States consistently fail to understand first, that there is no non-commoditized "family" left, no space in which love and goodwill can effectively substitute for monetary resources; and second, that traditional family space has been destroyed not by statists or liberal elitists but by the devastating operations of mobile capital and a "free" labor market.

The effect, in any affluent society where poverty is at the same time endemic, is to divide the social order into two parts and so destroy the sphere of "opportunity." Where the informal ideologies of civil society and the formal ideologies of the state (e.g., what is taught to children about "good" and "bad" in public schools) emphasize an overarching narrative of *individual* "success" and "failure," the result is a hierarchy of inclusion and exclusion.[4] The excluded come to be viewed as completely apart; as having, en masse, a behavioral problem or a genetic deficit or both: the familiar story of "blaming the victim."[5] Thus they form a separate caste, roughly defined by the intertwined fates of class, gender, and ethnicity. As members of this caste, their needs are administered to by people who have never themselves been hungry; who do not have to sell their bodies to make a living; who have never failed to receive medical care or a job interview because they (or their parents) lacked the resources to get to where it was being offered on time, or they didn't have the right papers; who haven't had their schooling constantly interrupted by malnourishment, illness, or sleeplessness.

To this administrative class the excluded are not only a bad example but a threat: "one paycheck away." To bring home the example and deemphasize the threat, the institutions of state and society—legislators, judges, and administrators—create boundaries between the excluded and

45

everyone else; sharp lines that highlight the delegitimation of the former. The cumulativeness of initial childhood inequality is therefore not only individual but institutional as well.

So the state becomes in reality a class state. The poor regularly go to jail for offenses that would earn the well-off a slap on the wrist or a counseling session; even worse, they are far more likely to be found (via involuntary commitment) in mental hospitals. As Parenti notes again, "the number of people involuntarily confined in American mental hospitals is twice the number of all . . . prisoners," and they are without even the "legal protections . . . afforded ordinary criminals." Taken together, these institutions are to a great extent little more than, in the words of Sister Elaine Roulet of the Bedford Hills prison for women, "public housing for the poor." So too, children get taken away from parents whose sole crime is being too poor to provide the material well-being and stability that even completely uncaring middle-class families can provide without any effort at all; so too a woman who sells her body too cheaply becomes an offender, although if she sold it expensively enough she would become a tabloid heroine. All in all, this class content of the supposedly neutral state was encapsulated most strikingly (though unintentionally) by Supreme Court Justice Potter Stewart, in his dictum that *indigency,* unlike "race" or "gender," is not a constitutionally suspect category. It is rational, not discriminatory, to exclude the poor from receiving social benefits that others may easily obtain.[6]

As well, everywhere that social stratification has a gender component (that is, *literally* everywhere) or a racial component, these elements are inextricably woven together. Members of various ethnic minorities are most likely to be poor, and so the class state also becomes a racial state. In the United States, where the perception of racial division is probably stronger than anywhere else in the advanced capitalist world, the racial state is concomitantly more visibly manifest. The favorite recreational drug of well-off white people, when used in its cheaper and more accessible form predominantly by poor black people, can earn the latter imprisonment for life. The "war on drugs" is in every way a war on the poor *and* the nonwhite; the "war on crime" is primarily a way of warehousing black men who can't support themselves legitimately; capital punishment is reserved primarily for those (mostly poor, disproportionately nonwhite, very often physically or mentally impaired, and almost always male) who can't find anyone of substance to defend them. Blackness itself is treated as a pathology, so that perfectly well-dressed black men (and even black women) will be followed around department stores by store detectives or harassed or even beaten (or killed) by policemen on only the vaguest suspicion.

The state also becomes, notoriously, a gendered state. Despite the American Supreme Court's recent discovery of gender inequality, it is still the rule (found everywhere around the globe) that a man who kills his wife in "a fit of temper" after terrorizing her for years did not "intend" or "plan" homicide; whereas the wife who, unable to defend herself against his terror in the ordinary masculine way, strikes back while his back is turned or he is asleep, is seen to have "planned" the crime and thus is likely to be charged with first-degree murder. A man may still successfully defend himself against a charge of rape by claiming he had reason to believe his victim was a "slut," or really "wanted it"; the woman's perception that she had said "no" and meant "no" has no equivalent standing, given the governing definition of "intent." Perhaps the ultimate revelation of legal "non-discrimination" is that well-off white men in various professions can use cocaine regularly with impunity, but poor women may go to prison for carrying a nickel bag of marijuana for their boyfriends.[7] But at much less drastic levels of inequity, as in the way that welfarist institutions themselves work, the capitalist state is almost everywhere a gendered state. In the simplest sense, women are not only permitted but encouraged to be dependent on men, but they are treated as less than equals if they become dependent on the state.[8]

In sum, in a system of cumulative inequalities, many people are confronted daily by institutions so opaque and by threats to well-being so immediate and unavoidable that to say they are not subject to discrimination is to torture words beyond repair. "The law" may be formally available to all on an equal basis, but it is most helpful to those who never need it; or who encounter it only in "civil" circumstances under which its blessings can essentially be purchased; or who are the beneficiaries of its fundamental assumptions. What is missing from the formalistic notion of discrimination is the simple realism of Anatole France's observation, now more than a century old, that "The law of France in its majesty forbids rich and poor alike to beg bread in the streets or to sleep under bridges." Or in William Blake's terser formulation, "One law for the lion and the ox is oppression."

For all these reasons egalitarian thinking since at least the time of Mill has steadily moved in the direction of expanding opportunity beyond the merely formal legal realm. To take another salient example, in the period of capitalist expansion in the United States, according to the Supreme Court the rights of labor were limited to "freedom of contract." This meant in principle that employers were free to offer jobs and individual laborers free to accept them; and in practice meant that workers, lacking the means to tide them over between jobs, had no rights at all (except to be abstractly "free to choose"). The New Deal and the New Deal–era Supreme Court that ratified its legislation recognized instead that individual rights could only be realized through the institution of collective bargaining. First in Section 7a of the National Recovery Act and then in the National Labor Relations Act and the Fair Labor Standards Act the laws were changed to ratify this more realistic sociopolitical understanding and to create new legal options for trade unions and their members. (Many of these, of course, have since been whittled away by subsequent legislation and unsympathetic courts).

Opportunity for members of the working class, that is, does not inhere in the possession of equal individual, legal rights; it inheres, to the extent that it exists, as part of a larger framework of trade unionization and the solidary power of collective bargaining. In the same way, opportunity for women inheres not in law reform but in changes in the customary assumptions that undergird the law of male supremacy; and opportunity for racial minorities can be realized only when the majority abolishes its own racial categorizations and thus the institutions of permanent white supremacy.

The institutions and understandings that define an arena in which equal opportunity is not merely formal but is in some serious degree realizable together make up a commitment to what I call *strong equal opportunity*.[9] To be sure, the commitment to individual rights (of social mobility and behavioral freedom) that defines traditional equal opportunity is the absolutely necessary base of the stronger conception. Strong equal opportunity is not, in other words, the opposite of or a substitute for equal opportunity in the traditional sense; but rather goes beyond the latter's formal, legal protections while continuing also to comprehend them.

To define strong equal opportunity, we have to begin by saying what it is not. Most fundamentally, equal opportunity (as I will call it from now on) does not mean equal rights to become someone who controls property in the means of production; that is, to become an employer of others. Since the average business employs many more people than it has real (that is, controlling) owners, most people by definition can never realize that "right." Even shareholders, in the land of mass shareholding, are a small proportion of the general population; and those within that group who actually get to dispose of the property in which they hold shares or to benefit significantly from its profits are a tiny minority within that minority. Abstractly, everyone has the "right" to become a capitalist; but very few people will ever be able to make that "right" a reality.

Equal opportunity is not about winning lotteries. Now, in finally attempting to give more specificity to Rousseau's formulation about those who can buy others, and those who must sell themselves, we can say rather what it is about. Equal opportunity is aimed at abolishing not only inherited privilege but also inherited disprivilege. It defines a social order in which no one's social background (including but not limited to their gender, economic class, and ethnic background), as distinguished from variations in individual taste and constitution, is likely in itself to exclude them from early development of the skills and attitudes necessary to qualify for socially useful and remunerative positions; in which no variety of reward conveys unchecked power over others; in which nothing considered a fundamental human good or necessity is distributed in such a skewed fashion that many people might just as well be said to have none of it (see my comments on old age on p. 19 above); and in which no such good is distributed in such a way that it can be passed on to some people's children while being unavailable to the children of others.

Equal opportunity in this strong sense would also mean that no small group of people, even if they possessed elite skills, could monopolize any important social good (including the public decision- making process); and that no large group of people would be excluded from access to any important social good (again, including the public decision-making process); while at the same time the development of the particular kinds of skill relevant to that society's values and needs (not just the values and needs of a particular social group) would be encouraged and rewarded. In any society so constituted—that is, in which all vestiges of both discrimination and institutionalized poverty had been eliminated—the purpose of both formal labor market policy *and* public and private institutions of training and employment would be to maximize the creation of positions requiring and rewarding the exercise of human capabilities to their fullest and to minimize the creation of positions that frustrate (more than temporarily) the development of human potential.[10]

Clearly strong equal opportunity is meritocratic by definition; it is also, I suggest, our intuitive response to the question of principle. Reverting for a moment to the New Found Land, surely the founding principle would be that only those who are able to do some socially useful task and yet *refuse* to do so might be excluded from the normal reward structure. No inheritance rules would be countenanced that would enable some people never to have to work hard, while others started out with nothing of their own and no institutions responsible for helping them onto the road to opportunity. Purely menial labor would likely be rotated to the greatest extent possible: what free persons would deliberately set out to create a menial class? By the same token free women, as I've noted, would not agree to any division of labor that traded off significant portions of their freedom for a monopoly of parenting; they would not agree to take care of the children while the men ran around multiplying their property holdings on terms defined by themselves; nor would they agree to any set of rules that explicitly or implicitly made them subordinate to their male partners.

Having said this, we can now see the radical implication of the notion of strong equal opportunity. It is that the rules establishing and governing the division of labor can't justly be determined by those who already have accumulated property and power. Rules about both the industrial and the sexual division of labor must be settled and enforced, *by general agreement, before* anyone can say who "deserves" what they have. Meritocracy can only come into existence on the heels of equality; without at least the extent of equality envisioned by the principle of strong equal opportunity, there can be no "merit" at all, but merely the "right" of the strongest.

Equal Opportunity and Democracy

Equal opportunity is ultimately an unattainable goal, however, unless it is founded in political institutions that guarantee *equal voice*, which is indeed but another term for "equal *political* opportunity."[11] How can we define this concept more meaningfully?[12]

We should begin at the beginning. "Everybody to count for one, nobody to count for more than one," John Stuart

Mill's summation of Jeremy Bentham's utilitarianism, is also the implicit slogan of all self-styled democratic government; the formal realization of political equality. However, to demand the equal counting of persons is only to begin the discussion of democratic equality. What does it mean to "count"? To be counted? To count for more or less than one? Certainly, mere legal possession of the vote in no way guarantees political equality. Neither representative government (which is produced by the right to be counted), nor majority rule (which actuates representative government) themselves ensure that citizens shall have an equal say or be equally able to hold officials to account. On the contrary, that kind of government can as easily institutionalize political *in*equality, devolving into rule by a stratum of ambitious, typically male careerists in a kind of elective and appointive oligarchy. If we think of the act of voting as the political labor that the mass of citizens engage in, then the relationship of voter to representative (and to all those officials whom representatives appoint) all too obviously mimics the relationship of factory worker to factory owner, to which Marx gave the familiar designation "alienated labor." The moment in which we install our representatives in office is the moment in which they have passed out of our control—and potentially into somebody else's.

Again, however, literally equal participation—that is, pure or direct democracy—is impossible in a complex mass society. What equality commands here is rather equal access to the decision-making process. This means first that political decision-making institutions (a category that extends far beyond the merely elective offices) ought to be arranged so as to be always open to public scrutiny and controllable by constituent interests; in the words of E. E. Schattschneider, the most important function of political parties and an electoral system is to *"define the alternatives of public policy in such a way that the public can participate in the decision-making process."*[3] It means, correlatively, an equal chance for all persons not only to attain positions of public authority, but also, and more importantly, to be heard by whomever is in those positions. The opportunity to be heard is especially crucial in that no matter how frequently offices are rotated and (what is much more to the point) no matter how generously the notion of "public" responsibility and accountability is elaborated, most people never will nor can hold a public office any more than they will or can be owners or managers of corporations. But all people will at one time or another have interests or needs that they will want to articulate to someone in authority, and, having done so, will expect to be treated with the same care respect as anyone else would be.

The minimum requirements of a polity of equals, therefore, can be simply stated. First, to the extent that representation is always necessary, the holders of offices (elective and appointive both) should attempt to represent, and should be expected to attempt to represent in an open manner, both general social desires *and* the particular special needs of individuals or small groups. Second, having "an equal chance to be heard" means that every voice should be treated with equal respect and that officials should be equally accountable to every type of person who is affected by what they do. This implies especially that what counts as "public" or "political" or "social" is not predefined so as to exclude issues that have widespread ramifications; as, for example, what a man does to a woman in "their" home, even though anywhere else it would constitute criminal behavior, has typically been treated by the law and public policy as "private." Third, when there is conflict among equals the most numerous voices should, with one exception, prima facie sound the loudest; the desires for favor or dominance of a small elite, whatever its alleged importance, should count for nothing more than its mere numbers.

The exception, though, is that the notion of equal voice has other requirements than the triumph of the most numerous. Taking it seriously tells us that the public decision-making process in an egalitarian social order cannot be based on simple, straightforward majority rule, for majority rule all too easily becomes majority despotism. Of course no matter how much the space of public discussion is democratized, it can never be guaranteed that any particular policy debate will actually be *decided* in favor of anyone in particular. Still, what the notion of "equal minority rights" does entail is that the realized idea of appropriate channels for political action in the nation, the region, the county, the municipality, and the neighborhood should incorporate a diverse multitude of arenas for organized civic action and of legitimate jurisdictions for making, influencing, and resisting policy determinations.

So hearings about building a freeway through downtown Los Angeles have to be held in the affected areas, as well as in City Hall. People who live in the area that will be torn down have to be heard about the effect on their lives; urban planners who testify have to be asked what criteria they have used in balancing those effects against improved traffic patterns; if the residents cannot afford to procure their own expert witnesses, the state (or municipality) must pay for them. Examples like this, of course, could be multiplied a thousandfold. Every day somewhere in the United States a public policy hearing is being held, to which the people most decisively affected have not been invited; and at which those who have written or spoken on their behalf have not been asked to speak.

American political institutions as presently constituted may be democratic in some sense of the word; but they are absolutely not the institutions that would be created by equals who knew that any of them might some day be members of a marginalized minority group. The requirement of equal representation is that, whatever is finally done, there should be some decision-making institutions open to everyone and all of those should ultimately at least be *equally visible and accountable* to everyone. A policy decision made in full knowledge that someone's needs will be ignored or impaired may be legitimate (after all, it's a rare policy that doesn't hurt anyone); a policy decision made in ignorance of those needs and in the absence of their expression can never be fully legitimate.

It's reasonable that those persons who, say, oppose a war that the majority favors should have to march on Washington, or barricade the Boulevard Saint-Germain, or mass at Trafalgar Square to be heard. But it is not reasonable that the poor, persons of color, women, gay people should have to march on Washington to secure equal attention to their needs; for, as I. F. Stone famously remarked, "The rich march on Washington all the time." Who needs a million-man march when one phone call to the White House chief of staff will place the interests of a firm, a sector, or a class at the top of the agenda? In the same way, when the separable interests of white people, or of men, or of heterosexual persons are the unspoken context of political agendas, then persons of color, or women, or of a gay sexuality are always in the position of supplicants. Among equals no one would be in that position. The only legitimate outcome of democratic equality, as I have defined it here, is that a "minority" should be merely a random collection of voters who lost the last election but might win the next one; not an identifiable group of permanent outriders on the body politic. They lost not because they're gay, or black, or Jewish, or Arab and no one else will vote for people "like them" or their interests, but because their policy preferences were on this occasion the less popular preferences. This means, of course, that the *institutions* of equal representation and participation must already be rooted in a culture of equality; they cannot produce equality by themselves. In a culture of equality we would distinguish among political platforms because of the ideas they put forth or even our feelings of dislike for the particular people presenting those ideas, not because of our invidious attitudes about their social backgrounds or group identities.

With respect to equal political rights, it's also crucial to understand that in the realm of equal opportunity these cannot be conceived of merely as negative protections—as rights not to be treated exceptionally badly. In the first place, in an age when so much of everyone's lives is lived by turning electronic switches on and off, effective access to the media of mass communication is as important or sometimes even more important as access to a public hearing at city hall. Whoever controls the image in a world dominated by the mass communication of images ultimately controls that world; in this respect, the mass media as we know them are devices that distort our voices rather than reproduce them. Their very structure is incompatible with the structure of democratic citizenship: of genuine representation, of mutual linkage, of rotation in role and responsibility between those who represent and those who are represented. There is no way that the controllers of the mass image can ever be representative of any constituency or can ever engage in anything but alienating communication. When we are all reduced to being consumers of someone else's worldview, then we surrender our own experience of what is human, of what is necessary, to a concocted experience that is necessarily a lie and a sham: yet it is a lie and a sham that is also more vivid, more real, than our own devalued experiences.[14] If the mass media can't be abolished, at the very least they would have to be restructured in an egalitarian polity, so that real voices might take precedence over ideological fictions and the propaganda machines of "news" and "information"; and so that minority voices would, again, have the additional access they require to overcome the stereotyping and dismissal that renders them into a cultural "other" and makes their formally equal citizenship chimerical.[15]

In addition, political rights can also be conceived of as rights to fulfill (as much as they can be fulfilled) those distinctive needs that are often the very definition of one's status as a member of a minority. To be allowed to take a college class is not, for a hearing-impaired person, to be treated equally, unless the classroom or the person herself is provided with the technology necessary to carry out the ordinary tasks of a hearing student (provided that hearing students don't need to buy anything to carry out those same tasks). To be free in a European or North American society to submit scripts about Islamic life to television producers who define their role as producing entertainment for the average viewer is not to have anything resembling an equal freedom to give voice to one's distinctive being. For women to be free to participate in political meetings that are scheduled with no acknowledgement of their being subject to the "tyranny of domestic commitments," is to have an equal freedom to participate unequally.[16] If the traditional structures of male supremacy and white supremacy (in European and ex-European societies) are left in place on the grounds that they are really "neutral" in their effects, then what actually happens is that many people must demonstrate extraordinary ambition or force of personality to achieve positions that in the normal course of affairs are available to others of merely ordinary character and accomplishment.

Of course, this demand to meet the distinctive needs of minorities also has its own egalitarian limits. For example, freedom of religious worship, or of abstention from any worship at all, would commend itself to a company of strangers proposing to live together in equality; but the freedom to establish a mandatory religion would commend itself only to those who were already members of a single sect. Seen in this light, a Jew who asks that he be allowed to worship like anyone else, in a synagogue of his own choosing, has nothing morally in common with an ultra-Orthodox Jew who would deny that opportunity to people who call themselves "Jews" but whom he doesn't recognize as such; or with one who asks that Judaism be made the official state religion of wherever he lives. In the same way, a worker who asks for rights of common ownership or of common access to wealth-producing means of production has nothing morally in common with an owner who asks for "rights" of exclusive ownership that are absolutely recalcitrant "to the needy man." The rights of minorities and the rights of majorities, in the end, are not really all that distinct.

We can see this most clearly by making use of the late Christian Bay's important distinction between *rights*, which can in principle be vindicated for anyone without detracting from anyone else's exercise of them; and *privileges* (in the informal rather than formal legal sense), the exercise of which by one person always entails their refusal to someone else.[17]

Thus, most crucially, this distinction tells us that the opposition of traditional liberals to campaign spending limits or to publicly financed campaigns is based on a misapprehension. To make a speech on behalf of a candidate is a right everyone has, and can be vindicated for everyone (or at least for everyone through representatives of their choice). Even to make an appearance on television to support a candidate could be thought of as a right, if the time were assigned by lot to the spokespersons for various candidates. But the so-called right to *buy* television time is not a right at all, but a privilege. It is not merely a privilege available only to a particular subclass of persons, those with large amounts of money. Even worse, it is a privilege in the sense that every such sale of time establishes a *monopoly*. Any time one persons buys a television time slot, it is by definition unavailable to anyone else, just as though the state that grants licenses to the owners of television stations (or networks) had granted some private person an exclusive monopoly to sell salt.[18]

In short, to be able to vote for the candidate of one's choice is a right; the exercise of that right detracts from no one else's ability to do the same. To be able to worship freely is to exercise a right; to have a religion certified as legitimate is to receive a privilege. To be able to call in a complaint to a television station is a right. To own the station is a privilege, and therefore to have an unique say over whose calls get taken seriously (not mine, not yours, but that of the public affairs representative from General Electric) is to have a privileged position, an unequal voice.

What equal political opportunity commands is that all voices should be able to speak freely and to make use of the same media for communicating their desires; that no voice should be regularly favored over any other; and that there should be channels of discourse available particularly to those who for historical or institutional reasons find it hard to "speak" or to make themselves heard. In principle, that is, just as the number of people who can vote should approach 100 percent, the number of people with personal access to the legislative chamber or any important locus of decision-making or opinion formation, if it is less than 100 percent, should diminish toward zero. Truly equal chances for everyone, but even more importantly, privileges for no one, is the essence of egalitarianism.

4) ACHIEVING EQUALITY

Surplus Inequality

ALL THESE DISTINCTIONS between real merit and its imitations, human rights and special privileges, what is earned and what is merely appropriated, are obvious once they have been spelled out. For this reason it is not conceivable that any people, having to work together to design their own institutions from scratch, for perpetuity, and with no interest in ideological obfuscation would design rules and institutions markedly different from the simple ones I have enunciated.[1] As Mill put it

> . . . society between human beings, except in the relation of master and slave, is manifestly impossible on any other footing than that the interests of all are to be consulted. Society between equals can only exist on the understanding that the interests of all are to be regarded equally. And since in all states of civilization, every person, except an absolute monarch, has equals, every one is obliged to live on these terms with somebody; and in every age some advance is made towards a state in which it will be impossible to live permanently on other terms with anybody. In this way people grow up unable to conceive as possible to them a state of total disregard for other people's interests.[2]

The sense of equality, of social solidarity, is part of ordinary human morality. If some other part of our being that conflicts with it, such as the desire to acquire property, is also ordinarily human, we cannot fail to recognize the conflict and will therefore have to grapple with it. The greater the proportion of us (explorers of the New Found Land, or whoever) that is engaged in that grappling, the more likely that the egalitarian sentiment will remain firmly rooted.[3] Even the most ardent libertarians, after all, are unable to escape this "understanding," for they insist that everyone has an *equal* right to pursue the acquisition of property. Pretending to deny the value of equality, they pay it homage instead.[4]

However, a complex industrial or postindustrial society is qualitatively different from a New Found Land. Posed as the question of fair rewards for work done, the argument for inequality is weak to the point of extinction. To that extent, we have already settled the matter of principle. There is no argument *in principle* favoring inequality; there is only the argument from utility. And this is a *political* argument, to be settled—as any political argument—in accordance with the majority view. Questions of *right* or *fairness* ought not, as I've indicated, to be settled by majority rule alone; that would be majority tyranny. But questions of policy—what should social goals be? how best to achieve them?—can be settled in no other way. There's no such thing as an objective social utility (or an objective individual utility) that can be announced with scientific detachment; the rationalistic language of economists when they speak of "utility functions" obscures the fact that these are nothing more than collections of individual states of mind.

But majorities also do not exist in abstraction. They have to be formed, and they are formed by people who listen to one argument or another and then, collectively, decide which argument is best. Therefore political arguments have in some way to be *good*, that is, persuasive, arguments. From this standpoint, the question of social utility is a much more difficult question for the egalitarian than the question of fairness. What's fair is a question that can be addressed, even if not definitively, by processes of moral reasoning. What are the effective incentives to get recognizably necessary work done and to maintain efficient productivity in general are questions that in the end can only be answered by making predictions—by educated guesswork.

Before trying to make predictions, we can at least establish what we really do know. We also have to clarify exactly what is the problem. It's not, for example, that we want to be sure there is the right number of brain surgeons—and in any event the free market is notably inefficient at meeting such specific requirements. Much more importantly, we want to maintain an appropriate mix in the production of goods and services, in the creation of social tasks requiring more or less skill, in the matching of unequally developed talents with those tasks, and above all in the encouragement of creative persons to develop new types of goods, services, or production processes. And the division of labor required to do all these things is so differentiated, the types of labor power to be drawn on by it so multifold, and the human groups providing that labor power so various in their social origins and backgrounds that it's virtually impossible to imagine any way of meeting these requirements except via the path of "private" enterprise: a "free"- -that is, capitalist—labor market and concomitantly, the inegalitarian and exploitative institution of wage labor. So we start from there: we can't simply wish this bedrock feature of capitalism away; we have to reason *from* it.[5]

Furthermore, since capitalism is a *structure* in which a few benefit unequally from the labor of many, our difficulty is not the relatively simple one of educating and training everyone up to their full capabilities, the mantra of neoliberalism. If that were the case, it would only be necessary to demonstrate the fraudulence of the sociobiological case for inequality and then to implement the narrowly drawn public policy of redistributing resources from wasteful expenditures to the educational system. But the genetic argument reoccurs and is received with respectful attention no matter how often attention is called to the scandal of its meretriciousness, pseudoscience, and intellectual dishonesty.[6]

This is because there is a much greater difficulty. Over time people living in advanced industrial societies have developed an incredibly differentiated structure of rewards and incentives. This structure's overt manifestation may be found every day in the daily newspaper's classified employment section. Here, hundreds of dead-end, menial industrial or service jobs rub shoulders with high-end technical or management openings requiring several advanced degrees and promising career opportunities that will eventuate in six-figure incomes. Many if not most of these jobs are defined in such a way as to make a significant gender differentiation (as in the requirement in some professions for the open-ended availability of the employee; or the specification of credentials that minorities or women are known not to possess in the same degree as white men).

Seen in this light, the entire empirical (or pseudoempirical) literature on "the causes of inequality" is a gigantic waste of academic time. It tells us nothing we didn't already know, namely, that the most outcast and denigrated members of a social order disproportionately fill its least rewarding job slots and its unemployment rolls. (In European societies with less social diversity and a deeper public commitment to relative economic equality than exists in the United States a greater proportion of the workers, male or female, needed to perform low-paying tasks are formally imported from abroad, rather than entering "illegally" as they do in the United States.) In addition, since unemployment insurance is a considerably less attractive option in the United States and also much less available, it tends to be replaced by petty crime and imprisonment among the worst off (e.g., black men). Prison and military service together take an immense number of people (especially black men) off the U.S. unemployment rolls, who would be on those rolls in less socially devastated and militarized societies.

Thus the workers who fill low-paying jobs aren't paid less because they lack "human capital" (i.e., appropriate moral attitudes) or are ill trained, although that may well describe their condition. On the contrary, usually they earn less because they belong to some group the members of which have been designated by historical circumstances and political weakness as being appropriate for the informal but very real classification of "lower"; and if some lack "human capital" (far fewer than superficial observation would suggest) that's because from an early age they've had no reason to believe that possessing it would do them any good. Most of the jobs filled by the members of these groups are low paying because their productivity is low (by conventional measurements), and given the structuring of a capitalist labor market, the reward for doing those jobs would be relatively wretched no matter the actual distribution of "human capital."

To complete this vicious circle, the gap between this low-wage work and higher-wage work is so large, and the resources devoted to bridging that gap so infinitesimal, that low-paid workers have little hope of obtaining the kinds of training that would enable them to better themselves.[7] In particular, a tremendous number of ill-paying jobs are really a substitute for domestic service: preparing food, washing up, sweeping floors, doing laundry, running errands, emptying bedpans, etc. (Or being a "welfare mother," the most ill-paid job of all). The problem for prospective employers is to find people to fill these jobs; better education or training for those in that potential job pool would be not a "solution" to that problem but instead an obstacle to its solution. If there were no high-school "dropouts," there would be a social disaster.

In addition, the best way to insure that there will not be a general revolt against a system that multiplies demeaning work is to make certain that those who do the worst on the labor market tend to be a definable minority, such as a "racial" or sexual minority. From the job market standpoint this is a sensible rationing device, nothing more. Therefore, the argument (made by economists such as Milton Friedman) that antidiscrimination laws are "irrational" because employers will always want to hire the most efficient workers available is the exact opposite of the truth. Even in times of labor shortage, there are more applicants in almost any distinguishable job pool than there are positions to be filled. The most important consideration for anyone engaged in supervising hiring practices is therefore the saving of time and effort. Unless minority applicants—or women—are noticeably "better" than their competitors, it is perfectly "rational," and in every way expectable, to simplify applicant selection by moving them to the end of the line (or out of it altogether).

The same pattern holds as well at the other end of the income scale. In order to economize on resources devoted to education and training, all social institutions and elite actors have collaborated beforehand to ensure that the best prepared are those who need preparation the least. The children of the well-off go to schools that spend more money per pupil on students who don't need nearly as much spent on them. They advance by taking tests that purport to measure "aptitude" but for which their entire lives are a training and a support. They receive alumni preference ("affirmative action") at institutions of higher education; benefit from various networks when on the job market; and if they are white males suffer from no stereotypes or informal glass ceilings enforced by people who think of them as "different." All in all, then, as Rousseau's remark suggests, whatever "natural inequalities" may exist among us are overwhelmed by the persistence of structured and designed inequalities that take on an aura of inevitability only because, after they have been in place for a long while, it would require so much effort to overturn them. The labor market thus becomes host to a vicious circle of such discriminatory "rationality."

All this being the case, the same free labor market that makes differentiated growth possible also necessarily casts thousands or millions of people by the wayside, and the more so, the more diverse and the less solidary the social order. Concomitantly, therefore, in any such society any putative agreement on basic principles of (strong) "equal opportunity" or a meaningfully equal chance at birth for all citizens would have to be translated into an extensive set of intrusive, bureaucratic, and in principle coercive institutions designed to help repair the damage wrought upon those persons by the inflexible labor market. Otherwise it would turn out to be a formalistic, empty promise: "equal opportunity" with neither equality nor even opportunity for millions.

We can think now of the inequalities produced by all these imbalances of social power as *surplus inequality*, inequality above and beyond the necessary inequalities of a complex division of labor, existing primarily to enhance the power and well-being of some people at the expense of others.[8] In an advanced capitalist society, the very principles of its organization generate surplus inequality and thus also create the need for institutions and policies of compensation and redistribution. By "compensation" I mean redress for acts of discrimination that violate the universally (in the United States) accepted principle of formal, legal, equal opportunity; these are addressed separately in chapter 6. Strong equal opportunity, in other words, does not in any way repudiate the more conventional version, but rather builds on and extends it. As to redistribution that goes beyond equal opportunity as conventionally understood, I do not intend to argue that particular institutions and policies are "good" or "right" in some objective sense. For anyone who finds the goal of equal opportunity compelling, however, these are the institutions and policies that we might propose to realize that goal.

The discussion that follows is meant to be neither all-inclusive nor definitive: not a package for the subscription of either readers or activists, but a strong suggestion as to what we would probably have to do to eliminate surplus inequality and institute equal opportunity. It is also addressed only to the question of equal opportunity, and it therefore ignores such general needs as those for military protection, municipal services, environmental preservation, etc. All that having been said, we now have to ask what, at a minimum, would seem to be the redistributive institutions and policies necessary for moving away from this gross surplus inequality and toward more equality and fairness?

Surplus Inequality and Redistribution

To answer that question, we have to define redistribution more carefully. The term has two connotations. The first, a permanent change in patterns of reward for doing social labor (or of compensation for not being able to do it), is what is most commonly meant. Redistribution can also mean a change in *structures of power*, however; these are at least as crucial and more decisively revolutionary in the long run. We begin, though, with a more conventional and familiar account of the kinds of redistribution that strong equal opportunity necessitates. These are, first, what its opponents (and once upon a time its friends) called "leveling," or the redistribution downward, of wealth; this is redistribution through progressive taxation. Second, "redistribution" also generally refers to the politics of the "welfare state," even if the revenue system that funds it is not all that progressive. Here "redistribution" is really used as shorthand for the aggregate of those policies that provide economic security by removing the provision of certain goods and services from the vagaries of "the market"; what has been redistributed is the way in which the necessities of human life are made available to the needy, who can now obtain them even without being able to "afford" them.

Even in this its conventional form, there are still two sharply opposed ways of conceiving the "welfare state." One, familiar to us as the "safety net" model, is configured not to lessen (let alone abolish) economic inequalities but to maintain them. The motives behind its creation had as much to do with the maintenance of social order as with a striving for social justice. Except, moreover, with respect to old age insurance—the recipients of which in the United States not only potentially form a powerful voting bloc but are also visibly ourselves at a later point in our lives—the impulses it evinces in operation are often those of disdainful charity and (especially but not only in the United States) sadism. We can best analogize this "safety net" to private sector charity. If I buy a hungry person a meal, I have momentarily assuaged her hunger, but she remains someone who is unable to feed herself (and if I spit on her while doing so I am behaving like many welfare officials). When we dispense aid to poor women with dependent children, their lives and those of their children are to some extent kept from falling into the most abysmal pits of despair: but they remain poor women and poor children.[9]

In an already egalitarian society, in which every non-criminal citizen was guaranteed access to essential goods and services, something not much more extensive than the "safety net" might well comprehend all the redistributive social insurance necessary. It would redistribute income from the lucky to the unlucky (e.g., the seriously or chronically ill) and, as suggested above, from those neither requiring nor giving care to those requiring or giving it. But the dramatic inequalities of contemporary capitalism require much more than that by way of rectification, or they will merely replicate themselves (and multiply themselves) over time.

A quite different notion of the "welfare state," often thought of as the Swedish model, has as its purpose not the maintenance of the poor but the abolition of poverty. In Sweden, "cradle to grave" universal programs of social insurance, including extraordinarily high levels of unemployment compensation and sick pay, are combined with particular support networks for those with special needs (e.g., the disabled or impaired, parents of young children), to ensure that no one can fall through the cracks of an affluent society; and that within the limits of a capitalist division of labor the opportunity to do whatever they can do is truly available to all persons.[10] The spirit of this welfare state (if not always its accomplishment) is indeed egalitarian (see ch. 7 below); whereas the spirit of the former is inegalitarian (we dispense charity to our inferiors, not to our equals). For reasons made plain by the quotation from Michael Parenti on p. 44, the abolition of poverty, or more generally of socially structured disadvantage, is the sine qua non of strong equal opportunity. Poverty—"the failure of basic capabilities to reach certain minimally acceptable levels"— uniquely multiplies "illfare."[11]

The most devastating inequalities of all are those occasioned by the kinds of childhood disabilities that cripple low-income parents financially and may weaken children's earning capacities for good. In particular, a great many women stereotyped as "welfare mothers" are actually just ordinary women trying to deal with impossible parenting demands on their own and are unable to afford any kind of parenting substitute such as the well-off take for granted. But almost as devastating for adults are simple bad luck on the job market (being in the wrong firm or the wrong sector at the wrong time), inability to realize savings from one's earnings, and above all, ill health. The last is especially crucial, in that the people with the most extensive chronic health care needs are almost invariably the people who can least afford to pay a market price for them.

To be sure, the contours of the welfare state are not a given, but an outcome of particular national histories. For example, as a 1997 report from the National Priorities Project's *America at a Glance* series matter-of-factly points out, the number of children not covered by health insurance in the United States is approximately ten million; the number of children not covered by health insurance in Western Europe is zero.[12] In this light, American history and culture have a clearly subjective component; the same thing is true of political institutions.

There is a political dimension to cultural differences as well. The difference between the relative acquiescence of

American workers to cutbacks in the welfare state and the mass rebellion of French workers against similar cutbacks is only partially explained by different traditions of working-class action and organization. It is also explained by the resentment that is bred by an American welfare state based on selective coverage and means tests, as opposed to the much broader-based support generated by one based on principles of universal coverage. (The political untouchability of Social Security in the United States makes the same point, though even this is now under siege.)

Thus the redistributive activities of the state are not derived from some objective model of either fairness or necessity, nor does any particular person such as myself have any warrant to treat them as such. They are rather the result of what people demand; of nonnegotiable claims addressed to perceived exclusion and neglect. The true meaning of "universal" here, however, is not that a web of transfer payments covers every nook and cranny of the body politic. Rather, the point is that the free market is everywhere understood as a second-best (at most) way of accommodating certain basic human needs. The so-called welfare state, however institutionalized and however financed, is more usefully understood as shorthand for any appropriate way of taking the provision of those needs "off the market."

In that sense, the manifest desirability of, say, universal prepaid health insurance, from the standpoint of ordinary human beings (at the very least for children) transcends cultural subjectivity. The evidence is plentiful that when it is on offer, people as a whole eagerly grasp at it. Moreover, the evidence is also plentiful that for distributing medical care in the light of its own purposes—that is, according to medical need rather than ability to pay—universal health insurance works better than any alternative system. In that light, and taking the nations of Western capitalism as a whole, we can deduce from the activities of those who are or have been subject to exclusion and neglect (not at the present moment a majority of all citizens), that the real historical claims and demands of organized people include at least the following: claims and demands for "taking off the market" health care, through some form of universal health insurance; financial security, in the form of effective basic income guarantees not limited to unemployment insurance and old-age pensions but comprehending also the needs of those who don't work for wages; assistance with the demands of child care, in the form of child support at a level designed to prevent childhood poverty; and assistance in caregiving generally, through subsidies to support it.

These nonmarket provisions may thus be thought of as fundamental to any institutions designed to compensate systematically for the unavoidable side effects of labor market inequality and of the gendered division of labor. As I've noted the list is hardly inclusive. The general point is simply that until and unless drastic inequalities disappear, the threatened Swedish model of social democracy, which would indeed be an unparalleled blessing for millions of Americans, is even so not a maximal but a minimal requirement of equal opportunity.[13]

The problem of "the welfare trap" may necessitate time limits on income provision, upper boundaries on child support, and so on. But the meaning of such limits in a social order committed to equal opportunity (to job provision for all those who seek waged work and basic income support for all those who have good reason not to seek it) would be quite different than the abolition of "welfare" in the contemporary United States and Great Britain, which simply casts millions of persons onto the scrap heap of history. Where illfare is not allowed to multiply itself and poverty is therefore not both systemic and largely hopeless, the formation of an apparently dependent class that becomes the object of social spite is unlikely to occur.

So too, a minimal requirement for equal opportunity is a redistributive model of educational opportunity—which, unfortunately, exists nowhere. The United States has what is probably the world's best system of mass public education. Yet if we compare the endowments of the Ivy League universities, Seven Sisters colleges, etc. with the resources of community colleges, many public universities, and especially teacher training colleges; or the pay of professors who specialize in graduate education with that of teachers in the elementary schools; or of teachers at the best prep schools with teachers at those public high schools with the most "at risk" students, we consistently discover an inversion of the principle that needed goods should be distributed according to need. The least needy have the most spent on themselves; the most needy (unless they manage to get themselves stigmatized as "special needs" students), the least. And generally speaking, it is overwhelmingly true that those who provide services for young people are paid less than the social norm. Equal opportunity would self-evidently require that this inverted pattern be set right side up.

Work

The abolition of those material conditions that make equal opportunity a meaningless slogan for large classes of people is the necessary underpinning of an egalitarian social policy; but it is not sufficient. In a way, we can say that the abolition of those conditions (together with the primary abolition of discrimination, of traditional, formal, equal opportunity) makes possible the realization of the "socialist" principle: from each according to their ability, to each according to their work. For that principle to be not only possible but feasible, the question of work itself has to be addressed. That is, if work is the primary path to reward (as "need" is the primary path to care), what is to be considered as "work", and how is work, whatever it is, to be secured?

At this point—that is, once we move beyond the Swedish model—egalitarianism can only be speculative. Unlike the redistribution of income or wealth, unlike the securing of welfare needs and basic labor market equality, and unlike control over working conditions "on the shop floor," drastic changes in the nature of general work life have never yet been the subject of organized popular demands. On the other hand, it seems safe to say that if and when equality demands move beyond the welfare state, reconceptualization of work life is almost certainly the direction in which people are likely to move.

With regard to the question of what is to be considered as work, some familiar issues, although interesting in their own right, are not really central to the conception of equal opportunity. Especially, both the social evaluation of particular careers and the social evaluation of work effort within those careers are questions primarily of cultural ethos and only secondarily of social justice. Is a poet "working"? How many hours a day does a poet have to write poetry in order to be considered a working poet? Must she have another "job" and write poetry on the side, as is mostly the case today? Should a seventy-word-per-minute typist be paid as much as a one hundred ten-word-per-minute typist? What ought to be the hardship pay of a deep-sea diver or a deep seam coal miner?

There are only two ways to answer such questions. First,

we can leave it to "the market" to decide them; or second, the public, through some kind of decision-making agency that is intended to aggregate tastes and standards (see p. 35 above), can do so. As a generality, we can say that the labor market process is most defensible the closer the socialist principle already is to being realized. That is, if we really are rewarding work rather than people's antecedent positions as possessors of capital or of special skills in a highly stratified labor market, then it is both practical and reasonable to let dollars "vote" instead of people. The power of the dollar only violates the standard of equal opportunity when some people have many dollars and others have virtually none.

In this respect, the only evaluation of "career" that can *never* be left to the market is the social evaluation of motherhood and homemaking. The reason for this is not that women overall are a minority, although at any one time the women fulfilling those roles certainly are one. It is rather that "the market" in this case has not only a history of prior discrimination (possibly we could say that about poets as well), but is itself founded upon and effectively derives its reward schedule from the treatment of those women as non-workers. If women had to be paid a living wage for becoming mothers and behaving like mothers—that is, for "producing" future workers and citizens—then the way in which we pay men and women for work done outside the home would have to change drastically. The capitalist "free" labor market, after all, is predicated upon a historical settlement that freed the institutions of accumulation (limited liability corporations) from having to take responsibility for the reproduction of "their" work force. That responsibility, unasked for and uncompensated, was thrust upon "the family"; but really it fell upon women. Because of this history, the question how much is "deserved" by a mother working as a mother in her place of residence can only be settled by "the market" *after* its existing foundation—that she (or on far fewer occasions a man who shares parenting with her) deserves nothing—has been overturned.

That foundation itself incorporates a contradiction: that "motherhood" is a glorious occupation; and that it is worth nothing. Women will approach equality with men, instead of being dependent on them (and therefore less than equal), only when the contradiction is resolved, and the "home market" is put on something resembling a competitive footing with the job market. This can be done partially by paying more for home work, in effect establishing basic needs support for it at the standard level of waged work; more crucially by splitting up home work, especially parenting, between women and men; and also by reevaluating the concept of "career," so that "transients" in the job market have as much opportunity for reward in it as its permanent (most likely male) inhabitants.[14]

To do any of this, of course, would not be nearly as simple as I make it sound. The gender division of labor is the one form of discrimination that in almost all modern societies remains justified as a matter of social principle. Even prejudice against sexual dissidents, although much more brutal, is recognized by all Americans, including those who practice and defend it, as potentially falling within the ambit of discrimination policy in the traditional sense. It has to be somehow justified as a clear-cut deviation from formal standards of equal treatment and equal citizenship; and those justifications, whether utilitarian or theological in their underlying orientation, are getting harder and harder to credit. So sexual bigotry today manifests the hysteria of the fanatic who, as Ambrose Bierce put it in *The Devil's Dictionary*, "redoubles his effort as his goal recedes."

Gender discrimination is different in that it appears or is made to appear by its proponents not as discrimination at all but as a more or less "natural" division of labor. The appearance, though, is only an appearance. The gender division of labor is sustained only by discriminatory labor market practices that deliberately restrict the work opportunities of women.[15] Until and unless those practices are finally abolished, "equality" is equality for men only: which is to say, not equality at all. Confrontation with the "gender question," therefore, is central to *any* conception of equal opportunity.

The second question, how is rewarded work to be secured, is also central to an understanding of equal opportunity. This is because the socialist principle all too obviously leaves open the ancillary question: *how should we treat people who aren't working* (by any standard at all)? Are they to be blamed for not having found work, or "rewarded" by a comfortable level of unemployment compensation for being victims of inevitable labor market fluctuations? The obvious difficulty here is that the more comfortable and long-term the compensation, the less the incentive to return to the world of paid work. Here "the welfare trap" seems to be inescapable.[16]

Again, this is a trade-off that can only be settled by the majority as a matter of social policy. But any social policy that penalizes nonemployment, or implicitly assumes that some kinds of "idling" are voluntary, has to be based on the assumption that at some point all persons who want work external to the household but have been unable to find it will be provided the opportunity to earn a genuine living wage: that is, a wage that enables a person to purchase average amounts of the goods and services considered necessary by a given collectivity of persons.

Equal opportunity, therefore, entails not only the recognition of domestic labor as a legitimate claim on income, but also some kind of (public or private) "employer of last resort" for nondomestic workers, if the socialist principle itself is not to become a new way of penalizing the unlucky. And in an egalitarian social order, moreover, the employer of last resort must provide serious employment, roughly equal in the opportunities it offers for advancement to average work in that social order. And it isn't as though we are talking about "make-work" either, about jobs that have to be only dead ends because the work they provide is basically useless. If there were an "employer of last resort" today, that employer—the public—would in fact genuinely require millions of workers to do recycling, urban rehabilitation, pollution control and environmental cleanup, the restoration of vacant land to productive use, alternative energy development and conservation, primary preventative and diagnostic health care, and, of course. training for all these and similar socially essential tasks.[17] Again, my purpose is not to provide a smorgasbord of policy proposals nor to solve the problem of public versus private allocation; and it is certainly not to suggest that all these useful tasks must be sponsored and financed by a central state. Rather, it is simply to point out how much basic work (in the United States but undoubtedly other societies as well) needs to be done that is not being done, and how much less devastating to millions of individuals and families even an unregulated labor market would be if needed jobs with a high public priority were provided and funded through a public labor market policy. In other words, not just essential goods (housing, health care) have to be "taken off the market"; so too does provision of the essential jobs that are needed to produce those goods.

Of perhaps equal concern is the question of what, regardless of whether jobs are available on the private *or* public labor market, is to become of those who would like to work as much as anyone else but can't, because full-time (or overtime) work is already monopolized by successful job-seekers and only part-time work is available? If paid labor is an occupation that we as individuals appropriately treat as our number-one priority, then by getting as much of it as we can we leave other values and occupations in the lurch.[18] Here we can't just shrug our shoulders and leave that determination to varying cultural judgments. A society of equals, however defined, can't leave the very value of equality itself to its own devices. Hardly anyone really disagrees with this argument; the only serious dispute is over what we mean by "equality." All American schoolchildren are taught to revere the Declaration of Independence and its hymn to equality, and most are asked to accept Lincoln's revision of it in the Gettysburg Address as part of their understanding and reverence. The cultural ethos of an egalitarian social order has to include the ethos of equality, or its concrete institutions will soon disappear.

In this particular case, therefore, equal opportunity demands a different set of cultural priorities from those that contemporary Americans are used to. The first priority of a truly egalitarian society is to make a "normal working day"—as determined by democratically expressed demand of all those who work—available to everyone who wants to do paid labor outside the home and is not presently engaged in some other, culturally acceptable and reasonably well-rewarded alternative to it, such as being educated or trained or raising children in the home. The second, but only the second, priority is fulfillment in work for everyone who seeks it. And this entails, almost certainly, a flattening out and shortening of what we now think of as the normal working day (for those employed by others). The redistribution of labor time is thus part of any advance toward more equality.

Correlatively, enforcement of collective bargaining procedures, together with occupational health and safety regulations far beyond those enforced by the much-maligned OSHA is the other major underpinning of a compensatory state. It is no accident that workmen's actions against the labor market and the English factory reforms associated with the name of Lord Shaftesbury together define popular and elite reaction to the early devastations of English capitalism.[19] The permanent institutions of male dominance aside, the central market inequality in any system of industrialized mass labor is that workers as individuals cannot resist the power of an employer who by force of law (often armed force) controls the labor power and thus the behavior of everyone around him.

Employers have virtually all the support of legal norms on their side. Primarily, only they can decide whether to open for business or not to open and how to deploy production processes. The best way to measure the extent of inequality in this system is to ask, first, how long does a business have to stay in operation in order to provide owners or top managers with a standard of living still incomparably greater than what some workers could earn in a lifetime of employment? For owners and chief executives of the largest-scale enterprises today, the answer is often that at any given moment if they shut up shop immediately all of them would have quite decent standards of living for the rest of their lives, and many of them would continue to live as plutocrats.

In addition, we might want to compare the incidence of occupation-related diseases and injuries between those two different groups. How many chief executives, we might wonder, have claimed workers' compensation for black lung disease, carpal tunnel syndrome, or spinal injury occasioned by heavy lifting? But this is a rhetorical question that answers itself as soon as it is asked. The obviousness of these comparisons is an index of the imbalance that collective bargaining itself and the protective institutions that organized labor moments insist on strive to rectify. The purpose of all of workers' collective action is to enforce reasonable pay scales, to resist the imposition of working conditions that shorten the work lives of employees or deplete their human powers, and to place restraints on the right of capital to do what it will with "its" property. Only collective bargaining strongly supported by legal and administrative norms on the one side and regulatory institutions coercively imposed on capital by the legislated political demands of the working class on the other side can accomplish this end. In their absence, workers are at the mercy of the charitable impulses of their employers; or else of the calculation of those employers that super-exploitation may be unprofitable in the long run. History gives no reason to believe that either the impulse or the calculation will be forthcoming with any regularity.

The welfare/insurance state, even in the advanced form I have been imagining, is thus generated by the normal operations of capitalism: that is, by a division of labor that as an ordinary matter multiplies welfare for the capitalist, managerial, and professional classes, and illfare for the working class, especially working-class women (who have less access to well-paying work and fewer resources when they are deserted by men). That some, even many people born into the working class eventually escape it does not modify this comparison. Whoever is going to inhabit them, there are millions more working-class *positions* than there are upper- and professional-class positions combined, and therefore equal opportunity in the form of upward social mobility can never be more than anecdotal at best. In the same way, the labor regulatory state is generated by the normal—and normative—division of power, as uncontrolled capital's built-in power to destroy lives is moderated so that it can only constrain them.

If the state is thus central in maintaining equality, the state itself must, as we've seen, be an egalitarian institution. (I refer here, of course, to all levels of legitimately coercive jurisdiction, national, regional or provincial, and local.) At first glance it might seem that political equality should be comparatively costless, in that the public financing of elections costs a good deal less than does the existing American system of privatized bribery. But as I've noted, equal voice requires a good deal more than the right to vote, write letters, and so forth. Real political equality requires that everyone with an interest (or their direct representatives) should actively be consulted, all opinions should be solicited, every public servant should be held accountable for official actions to every affected constituency, and political forums should be made available to people who don't ordinarily have easy access to public space. If all that is the case, then public policy-making will be hamstrung a great deal more by the equal rights of citizens even than would be corporate capital by the equal rights of labor. Moreover, there is a further, even more stringent requirement of political equality.

"Equal voice" is not an individualist abstraction, referring simply to the rights of the isolated individuals of liberal social theory. Equal political opportunity is in fact most especially at risk when the very notion of "the individual" is inverted. Through this historic inversion, immortal, disembodied corporations are treated as though "they" mobilize a nation's productive resources, and actually embodied human labor is treated as though it mobilizes nothing but its own fragile solidarity. In the United States, where governmental unity and party cohesiveness are less developed than in most other capitalist states, companies such as Archer Daniels Midland or Hercules Powder or innumerable others can, by contributing to political parties, buy favorable provisions in tax codes or hidden subsidies attached to completely unrelated legislation without anyone having the faintest idea that this is what is happening. What would be an illegal bribe when passed from one embodied person to another sheds its illegal but human nature and becomes simply a "contribution" from one disembodied entity to another. In this process, real individuals, families, or collectivities disappear and are replaced by the entirely fictive "persons" who wield effective power in capitalist societies.

Even in polities where political campaigns are publicly funded and parliamentary candidates are chosen by their parties rather than being individual adventurers on the make, the "needs" of business, which are expressed by nobody in particular, produce austerity programs that "tighten the belts" of real people who are already in a state of bodily need. It follows that everywhere welfare policies are made without consulting people suffering from deprivation; public health policy is made by people who go to private doctors; safety regulations are instituted by people who have never spent a work day at risk; land use policies are determined by planners and builders who aren't going to live on that land; the desirability of public housing is evaluated by people who live in detached houses in the suburbs; the law is administered by people who never have to appear before it. This is what it means to count for more than one; or less.

One person, one vote is the maxim of democracy; one dollar, one vote is the maxim of plutocracy. Since political equality is only possible where the public's effective access to decision-makers is dispersed rather than concentrated in a few hands, limiting the power of those corporate entities that dispose of immense wealth is the highest priority of democratic equality. However, we should not think of this as necessarily a prescription for centralized control over production processes or the delivery of services. Rather, it is again a requirement for accountability: in this case the accountability of those who exercise not formally institutionalized political power, but the equally compelling power that accrues to a small number of people on whom the rest of us are completely dependent for our material well-being.

More concretely then, what democratic equality demands is the effective abolition of the impermeable boundary that the practitioners and ideologists of market capitalism have created between "public" political institutions and the allegedly "private" realm of economic institutions. As long as that boundary stays firmly in place, those who purportedly represent us are barred from doing anything about the most important aspects of our collective lives. Democratic equality means extending practices of *public* accountability to the conditions under which we work, the effects of that work on the spaces within which we lead our lives, and above all to the disposition of the hundreds of billions of dollars of surplus wealth that our interchanges with them generate.

In sum, democratic equality requires that the real conditions of accountability today be totally reversed. Far from being unaccountable, corporate economic power should be subject to democratic control. And far from being effectively accountable to and dependent on "private" corporate power, elected or appointed officials should be accountable only to the various real people, one by one, owner or worker, who make up the artificial corporate body. This is probably not a live possibility, even though the overwhelming majority surely desires in principle that it should be so. But what is a live possibility is that in a democracy all of public law and public policy should try to make it so.

5) THE COSTS OF EQUALITY

The Big Trade-off?

I F A L L T H I S I S what egalitarianism ultimately might require, what would it cost? In the world of pseudoexpert commentary fashionable nowadays, *New York Times* reporters with no knowledge of the world beyond the abstractions of neoclassical economics and desultory interviews with national elites to whom they have introductions confidently pronounce the death of Swedish social democracy and of statist "sclerosis" in France and Italy. Meanwhile, the United States and Great Britain, societies which have witnessed a massive redistribution of wealth from the poor to the rich, are held up as models of the entrepreneurial spirit, which the rest of the world must emulate or die. To take perhaps the most telling figure: between 1983 and 1989 in the United States there was a transfer of marketable net worth, or household wealth, of 5 percent from the bottom 80 percent of the population to the top 1 percent; the bottom 80 percent lost a fifth of their net worth, the top 1 percent gained 15 percent. In absolute figures, in 1989 the top 1 percent of American households held 39 percent of the nation's net household wealth and 48 percent of its financial wealth. If this is what it takes to get wealth holders to do their alleged job of creating more wealth, it is surely the most incredible bribe—or extortion—in the history of the human race.[1] To use Arthur Okun's well-known term, is this "big trade-off" of equality for "efficiency" the necessity that it is alleged to be?[2] Is the spirit of equality so antithetical to progressive enterprise that any society in its thrall must either retreat to a noncompetitive world of local self- subsistent economies or become unable to survive in the global economy at a level of consumption near to what inhabitants of the modern world have come to expect?

In considering this question we can dispose of one conventional answer right away. Both economic theory and direct historical comparisons tell us that, other things being equal, greater degrees of inequality (as assessed by standard measures in use by contemporary economists) are *less* conducive to growth than lesser degrees of inequality. The recent boom in the U.S. economy does not affect the overall record. Whether the comparison is between the social democracies or more unmitigatedly free market economies; between nations in an earlier period of extreme inequalities and the contemporary period of constrained inequalities; or between recently developing nations such as South Korea or Taiwan on the one hand and Brazil and the Philipines on the other hand, the conclusion is the same. Most of the time the less unequal partner in the comparison has done better; and the abstract theory tells us that this is to be expected. Although there are several considerations at stake, generally speaking the case against inequality can be summed up by saying that more inequality means less popular consent, less consent means less stability for property rights and thus less security in the carrying on of enterprise. Less inegalitarian societies also spend more on education and health, thus generating and supporting a more productive labor force.[3]

Again, the case for inequality seems to stand on weak ground. Unfortunately, as this brief summary reveals, the literature does not answer, or even address, the question that Western egalitarians are really interested in. This question is not whether welfare states can "deliver the goods" as well as free market states. That issue has long since been settled, in practice as well as in theory. Through the second half of the twentieth century it was at least as easy to find something resembling a good life in Sweden as in the United States, and easier for a large proportion of the blue-collar working class. The quite different question egalitarians want to be able to answer—a question suggested by what is happening in countries such as Sweden, Germany, and France—is this: Is there some point in the growth of nations at which any further redistribution in favor of the less well-off would be economically harmful, so that no further redistribution beyond that point should be encouraged, and any that has already occurred will have to be cut back?

Questions like this, of course, are made not to be answered definitively; the best we can do is make educated guesses which are then passed off as "predictions." These guesses or predictions, too, are always distorted by the natural tendency to confuse current events with historical trends or even historical requirements. In the present instance, "the logic of globalization," the "crisis" (or "death") of the welfare state, etc., are being taken as revelations of some real economic necessity rather than as *revelations of the political power of international capital.* The "swollen" and "costly" French welfare state, in other words, is "swollen" and "costly" only by the standards of the European Economic Union's demands for a common currency, which requires cutting back public spending in those member states which exceed its coercive requirements. Once we understand "globalization" for what it really is, the momentarily unchecked power of an international capitalist class (and its regional and sectoral variations), we also understand that there is a world-defining (and perhaps world-shattering) difference between "efficiency" as a way of maintaining production to supply people's needs, and "efficiency" as a way of maintaining production to support the greatest possible capital accumulation for the smallest possible number of people. The former is a necessity of life; the latter is a necessity only of profit levels. This much having been said, we can then proceed to draw some necessary distinctions.

As we shall see, there are three kinds of redistribution demanded by the surplus penalties a capitalist economy imposes on those unfortunate enough not to be offering the trained skills its high- growth sectors require. First, there is redistributional taxation, either of income or of wealth, from the best-off in society to the worst-off. The limits to this process are clear, and are manifest in every capitalist nation today. Redistributive taxation on earned income belies the promise on which a capitalist society is based: the promise of unlimited acquisition. Or rather, this promise becomes the premise of life at a certain point in the natural history of capitalism.

In 1928 Herbert Hoover's slogan of "a chicken in every pot and two cars in every garage" could sound like an inspiring slogan, for the summit of aspiration for most people (in every capitalist nation) was simply to enter the world of economic advancement on any terms available. To achieve that goal in the wake of the Great Depression, across the Western world (including the United States) levels of progressive taxation were gradually instituted that now seem astonishing. Typically, the highest marginal bracket was set at around 90 percent (although given the tax avoidance of the wealthy these levels were more a sham than a reality).

Still, the unequivocal evidence of income statistics is that progressive taxation worked. In the middle third of the twentieth century egalitarian redistribution took place over an extended period, into the late 1970s in many nations. Nowhere, except perhaps in Northern Europe, was the working class as a whole truly embourgeoisified; but for the majority the status of Hoover's slogan gradually passed from bad joke to ordinary expectation.

Therefore, although the end of the great postwar boom brought cutbacks in real wage levels in all the Western industrial nations (and Japan as well), right-wing policy makers—with considerable help from the inescapable fantasizing of the American mass media—built on the boom with great success. They fashioned a counter-revolutionary transformation from an emphasis on democratic equality to an emphasis on pitilessly "free" markets in popular ideology; a transformation that begins to cross all boundaries. In this transformed political arena the practical goal for the non-poor, that is for most people, has come to be nothing more than to defend (often with little success) those wage levels. Beyond that our collective ideological imagination seeks not a subsistence income but comfort-oriented (if not luxury) consumption. In such a circumstance, the cost of a transformative welfare and educational system does come to seem immense, no matter how hard progressives try to cast them as "merely" redistributive.

In large measure, however, the cost seems so immense because real power and wealth have already, in most nations, been exempted from paying it. Real property taxes, the sales tax or value-added tax, and even the inheritance tax, often—not only in the United States, although certainly there—fall harder on people who have "worked for a living" than on the truly rich. The so-called middle class is aware of this fact for good reason. When in his most radical phase, Mill proposed a confiscatory inheritance tax, for example, inheritable property of any value was in the hands of very few people. Now, every middle-class person and many working-class people as well hope to leave an estate of some kind to their children; such a tax would appear as just another insult: and it would not seriously affect the truly wealthy.

A progressive wealth tax is certainly achievable, and can possibly be scaled in such a way and imposed on such carefully defined items (e.g., on homes assessed at over one million dollars, holdings in currency, jewelry, and objets d'art above a certain value) as not to feel like another imposition on the aggressively politicized middle classes. So too might a confiscatory tax on "earnings" (which often are simply appropriations by those with managerial or ownership powers) above a certain amount, as long as this was tied to a reduction in taxes for everyone else.[4] Politically, however, the most sharply defined tax on the wealthy and the tax most directly attuned to an egalitarian program that was also favorable to entrepreneurial activity would be a prohibitive tax on luxury spending and on speculative (i.e., short-term) capital gains; for the number of people in any contemporary society who have a lingering desire to purchase ocean-going yachts and private jets or to invest in derivatives is proportionally negligible. Combined with confiscatory taxes on fixed and inherited wealth above certain amounts and on "earnings" that have nothing to do with production, these would define a genuinely production-oriented egalitarianism. What those levels ought to be, political theory cannot say. Only the members of a political movement pursuing more equality can decide whether, say, interest flows of several million dollars a day to one family are "obscene." But the principle is straightforward. Wholly aside from disagreements over the absolute amount of taxation and over the appropriate beneficiaries of tax revenues (see below), most people find the idea that the wealthy should pay more than the nonwealthy both just and socially useful.

However, even if a taxation system could be made to seem painlessly progressive in the face of this counter-revolution of rising expectations, the costs of equality actually are greater and potentially more painful than a simple comparison of putative public spending budgets and tax revenues would suggest. The most expensive components of a true welfare state would be health care expenditures; the production of useful skills and knowledge for all; basic income support; and support for caregiving activities. As to the first, in the United States redistribution would not necessarily be a material as opposed to an ideological problem. Overall spending on health care might actually go down if an out-of-control privatized and only quasi-public health system were replaced by a genuine single-payer public insurance program. The administrators, insurers, etc., who derive the most benefit from the for-profit system would be big losers, but they would derive no sympathy from most users. Other things being equal, the public budget for health would increase with a shift from private to public financing, but the public's out-of-pocket expenses could be unchanged or might even fall; in the long run only anti-state propagandists would fail to understand this. There would of course be redistribution of care, from the well-off to the needy (regardless of class); however, the only income redistribution would be that already contained in a progressive tax schedule. (The wealthy, whoever they still might be, might actually pay less than is now the case, although on the other hand they would strive to create a separate private sector that would maximize both their care and their costs).

The second form of redistribution that equality requires is ultimately more extensive. The public's out-of-pocket expenditures and even our very perception of what living a private life is all about would be changed drastically by the income and infrastructural supports fundamental to an egalitarian state. This is clear enough with respect to the notions of income support for basic needs, of the revaluation of women's non-wage labor, and of an egalitarian focus on both early childhood education and higher education for general and special skills. Clearly, the more material and especially moral resources we concentrate on overall social welfare and especially on raising the collective floor, the less we have to give to smashing through our various individual ceilings in the usually vain hope of joining the luxury class. Putting this change in outlook together with the changes in caregiving required by the egalitarian principle, we confront a true revolution, even without the drama of abolishing divisions of labor, sovereign states, the exploitation of "nature," and the like.

That is to say, the most fundamental transformation required by such a change is *from an ethos of private commodity consumption to an ethos of public well-being consumption.* In other words, we would *all* have to engage in a massive transfer, not of our collective income but of our collective outgo, to buy the kinds of goods and services that no one is ever seriously advised in public to look for today. The economy that produces public goods (many of them not even commodities) would have to become central to our collective consciousness, and the private goods-producing sectors that are today its very core would have to become comparatively secondary. What we now are on the whole the least willing to pay serious money for—children's well-being, cleaning up people's dirt and attending to their pain, low-cost transportation to and from work—would become the core sector of the economy, full of high-tech support systems and wellpaid service suppliers. As I have noted earlier, what we today think of as unproductive expenditures we would have to re-envision as among the most productive expenditures of all.

To comprehend the extent of the change required, we might try to imagine a television system in which there were no visually brilliant sales pitches for cars, beer, detergents, software manufacturers, or the armed forces ("Be all that you can be"); but that instead the same creative energy went into heartwarming and visually exciting narratives of what our tax money accomplishes when spent on helping parents take care of their children, on school science projects ("be all that you can be"), or on well-appointed public housing. The extent to which any person sympathetic to the egalitarian project finds this a ridiculous let alone quixotic idea is a measure of the moral transformation we would all have to undergo. And even that transformation would be useless in the absence of a social movement determined also to transform the hierarchy of value, so that those who accumulate the most private capital would be replaced, at the top, by those who provide the most public benefit; and so that the distance between those at the top and everyone else would be decisively lessened.

Finally, one further aspect of this transformation, no matter how much we try to avoid thinking about it, is that for the inhabitants of the Western capitalist nations equal opportunity would also entail some redistribution from themselves, as a collectivity, to the poor peoples of the world. The non-Western nations that have done the best job of capitalist modernizing are those that have rejected an import substitution development strategy that strangles the growth of domestic industry (while improving the consumption of local elites), have not allowed their agricultural and mineral resources to be exploited at prices set by international monopolies (e.g., the OPEC boycott), and have instead opted for an export-led development strategy that enables them to compete with the developed world. The most successful of them—South Korea and Taiwan, notably—have also been recipients of massive amounts of development aid from the United States, as front-line states in what was once American cold-war strategy. Debt relief or restructuring (Mexico, Egypt, Morocco, Poland) has also benefited even some of the worst-off nations (e.g., Ghana) in contrast with their neighbors. In sum, revolutionary or reformist movements, whether from the socialist Left or the authoritarian nationalist Right (though perhaps not the reactionary religious Right), would emphasize domestic capital creation in the poorer countries and the reduction (or prohibition) of capital outflows; price rises in their basic commodities; and finally their competitive entry into world consumer good markets. Whatever else happened, consumers in the Western world (though less so in the United States than in the more foreign market–oriented EEC.) would face at least a short-run decline in their commodity standard of living.

Having said all this, we now have to remind ourselves what else we would be implying about human existence if and when we collectively set out to curtail the global power of private capital. The consumption of commodities, which capital provides in abundance even while distorting their distribution, is only one way of measuring living standards and far from the best way. Even the most vulgar materialist ought to prefer, say, life expectancy at birth as a measure of well-being or (inversely) working days lost to illness and injury. If "happiness" is the real standard, as it must be for any materialist, we don't have the faintest evidence that increments to material consumption increase it, once some culturally relevant threshhold of basic economic security is safely passed. "Of happiness and despair we have no measure," wrote Spinoza; only economists fail to understand this. Our monetary consumption of goods and services only measures our demand for goods and services with monetary prices attached to them; whether they do have a monetary price indicates not whether we value them but whether some form of them is saleable in an imperializing, mass consumption-oriented, capitalist marketplace. That people sell and buy babies is an index not of our valuation of human lives but of the extent of social disrepair.

It's quite possible, therefore, and perhaps even likely, that a straightforward redistribution of the social values we measure by price would increase the kinds of happiness that can't be measured: the enjoyment of social solidarity rather than fragmentation; the diminution of class envy and its obverse, fear and contempt; the supplanting of a culture of anxiety by one of relative security. This is not just a matter of aggregating individual amounts of happiness, either. The costs of maintaining an upper class, complete with golden parachutes that pay it the more the less it accomplishes, are immense. But they're not even a fraction of the concomitant costs (now increasing everywhere) of reproducing, maintaining, and often incarcerating a reserve army of labor and its children, who will never be allowed to become productive citizens. As the cross-national literature on equality suggests, it might well be that even by the most vulgar materialist standards of measurement, average productivity would rise rather than fall in a more egalitarian social order oriented toward the production of public goods and the development of human skills.[5]

In any event, it is also the case that there are different, and thoroughly incompatible, ways of assessing the aggregate of social happiness in the first place. Suppose, as an exercise in the moral imagination, that we could indeed measure happiness numerically, to our own satisfaction. Let us then think of some representative human societies as being divided into three broad and very abstractly conceived classes. (Therefore we must momentarily do what is inexcusable when social scientists do it and omit gender from our categorizations of class, as though every woman came permanently attached to a man). In society A, which we may think of as manifesting contemporary American tendencies in slightly exaggerated form, the most well-off class comprises one tenth of the population and boasts an average material well-being value, as measured by income, of "150" (150 of what, we will allow the economists to say). The middle class, half of society, has an average income of 25; and the least well-off, the remaining 40 percent, are so ridden by debt, disease, and incarceration that they are without real income: their lives deliver no positive material benefit. In this society the average income per person, it turns out, is 27.5, but considerably less than half the population is at or above this average, and considerably more than half the population is below the middle-class average of 25.

Contrastingly, in the more egalitarian society B (which has no contemporary analog, not even Sweden), the classes are of equal size (representing, perhaps, the most highly skilled, the least skilled, and those in between), poverty has been abolished, and the average material well-being (income) of the classes measures out at, respectively, 24, 21, and 18. The average income per person, obviously, is 21; two thirds of the population is at or above the average, and the remaining one third only slightly below it.

Now if we compare the two societies, it will seem that "on the average" the "standard of living" in A (27.5) is 30 percent higher than in society B (21); moreover, even the median income is a bit higher as well. In other words, if these "values" are convertible in the form of some global currency, then not only is the sum total of material well-being higher in A, but more people are materially better-off in absolute terms. At this point, though, the question, "which society is better?" can only be answered circularly; the same is true of the question "which society is more just"?

Instead of attempting to answer the unanswerable, readers of these words, most of whom will by the nature of American book publishing have (or if they are students will expect to have) incomes above the median, might want to ask the following: If I knew nothing else about these two societies (such as the kinds of cultural activity they manifest, their climates, etc.), except that they were typical advanced industrial societies of the late twentieth century, which would I want to live in? Or, if I lived in society B and had a choice, would I want to move to society A? Would I be unhappy if I couldn't move to A? Put simply: to the extent that option B even seems plausible, if not decisively preferable, we will have refuted the notion that more is always better, and that patterns of distribution, as opposed to the sum totals of income (and wealth), are irrelevant to our visions of the Good.

However, this can only be a semi-conclusion; it is only the beginning of an analysis of the costs of equality. Patterns of distribution, unfortunately, cannot be plucked out of the ether. People have to have worked up a material world before they can distribute its outputs or their exchange values; and they have to be able to work together to maintain, reproduce, and improve that material world for themselves and future generations. Only congenital ascetics will be tempted by the prospect of equality in poverty or by the life of a simple commodity, premodern, precapitalist society. Although there are quarters of the world (for example, village and rural India) where that kind of life might represent a great advance in well-being for the majority of people, the idea of communal self-sufficiency has little attraction for those of the world's peoples who live a commodified existence at the highest levels of material consumption. It may be that some day humanity's pillage of the earth will necessitate the making of such a choice, but we can't reason that far ahead of our time. At the moment, when we in the materially developed world speak of "more equality" we can only mean by it more equality within the framework of advanced economic development.

That being the case, distribution (since Aristotle the heart of the concept of "social justice") can only be a secondary practical concern, no matter what the moral or esthetic claims on us of particular distributional arrangements. Production and reproduction are the primary concern. To be sure, there are built-in limits to the value of growth. After all, it's up to the partisans of inequality to explain how we can have the kind of continual, unregulated accumulation that produces great wealth without despoliation of both the natural and man-made environment; how we can promulgate material consumption as a dominant way of life and yet not promulgate the consumption of drugs, sleaze, and cultural trash in general; and how we can legitimize greed as a way of life without legitimizing crime as a way of life.

On the other hand, egalitarianism has its own built-in limitations. Whatever skeptical thoughts we might share about the fetishism of growth, John Stuart Mill's contrary ideal of the "steady-state economy" is chimerical. A machine that is merely maintained is already running down. There is always something new that has to be done, and people who just want to keep everything the same will be unprepared to do it. Concretely, a society without entrepeneurs and the entrepeneurial spirit is a collection of people who are only marking time. Nor is it really feasible to say, "Well then, let's nurture a class of entrepeneurs who will be helpfully accommodating and have no desire to become an oligarchy." Who will nurture the nurturers? How can we respect a desire in others if we do not respect it in ourselves?

In other words, the question about society B isn't whether it sounds likeable. To believe that given a live option, people will prefer more equality to less equality doesn't in fact require much from the moral imagination. Only those who think, *contra* Mill, that the concepts of empathy, mutual respect, and care for others are sentimental drivel compared to the hard-nosed reality of self-regarding materialism will certainly reject that belief; but then, as I've suggested earlier, moral imagination is exactly what they lack.[6] Our question is whether society B sounds possible. That is, egalitarians must believe in the first instance that a social order dedicated to more equality and less accumulation of capital in private hands can deliver the necessary goods. We already know that brutally inegalitarian societies such as the United States and England can do this; that we may detest the degree of inequality manifest in them doesn't change the facts.

It has to be emphasized, furthermore, that in speaking of equal opportunity we're not just talking about choosing butter over guns in the federal budget, enabling more black teenagers to graduate high school and go to college, delivering more public health care for the needy and less gratuitous private care for the wealthy, and so on. All these things can be done, and the United States (or England) would then look more like a Scandinavian country or Holland. But as the preceding analysis has demonstrated, creating a better welfare state is only the tip of the egalitarian iceberg. In any event, the Northern European countries are having difficulty in maintaining their relatively generous levels of public provision, precisely because of the pressures on them to maintain competitive productivity once they accept the logic of private accumulation.

The Question of Incentives

What we have been considering here goes well beyond the welfare state model. It is a kind of equal opportunity that promises not only basic well-being for all but an equal chance for everyone to realize their potential positive capabilities; and to share in the exercise of public decision-making rather than being nothing more than its object (except, feebly, on election day). And what we have seen is that none of this can happen without the unequivocal taming of corporate wealth, power, and privilege: the wealth that unendingly multiplies itself; the power of abstract capital to make and remake the world to its own needs regardless of the effect on concrete persons; the privilege of its owners, controllers, and servants to exercise a kind of influence and live a kind of life unknown to most other people.

We are trying, that is, to imagine a world in which economic actors who must necessarily be aggressive are asked to deliver their goods from the standpoint of the general welfare rather than, or at least as well as, merely their own; in which the striving for unlimited acquisition and unlimited social power that economic success seems to produce in its wake are rigorously curtailed; and in which men view women as full-fledged human beings rather than primarily as domestic servants. Can such a world generate and sustain useful entrepeneurial activity on a mass scale? We want to know, that is, if there are credible incentives to creative economic activity that aren't utterly self-regarding and gender-specific and whether the acquisitive spirit can ever be expected to produce a drive for limited rather than unlimited acquisition. Although these too are unanswerable questions, there are two important considerations on the side of an affirmative answer to them.

The first of these is that we must never think of socalled incentives to economic behavior in the abstract. Like other social behaviors, incentives have to be learned. There may be a universal impulse to get what one can, but the operative modifier is "what one can." What is available to be sought, lusted after, recklessly pursued, is always culturally determined. Whatever those objects may be, they always come encased in internalized limitations and prohibitions; those who fail to internalize the limitations and prohibitions are known as criminals or sociopaths.

With respect to prohibitions, for example, many soldiers who spend some of their available time abroad exploiting and occasionally raping indigenous (what the military calls "native") women will intend to be faithfully monogamous when they return home to their families. They don't behave differently abroad because they are "innately rapists" at last free to do what they really want to do but because the culture of the military defines what they do as "not rape," as an understandable and permissible "letting go" with women who don't really count as women, and then looks the other way when they do it. They don't do what they know to be a crime, but given the hint that a potentially pleasurable behavior is not criminal, their social behavior changes. It is not their personalities that have changed but their temporary, enculturated, understanding of what kind of behavior is legitimate. Men who don't want to think of themselves as rapists will not want to engage in any activity that they understand to be classified as rape.

In games as in sexual behavior, context determines behavior. Serious chess players, for example, don't cheat; there's little opportunity and it would destroy the purpose of the game that they play out of love as well as ambition. They do everything they can to intimidate, though, going well beyond the boundaries of what in noncompetitive contexts would be considered appropriate social behavior. Tamerlane was no more ruthless than Bobby Fischer; he just had a larger board on which to play. Serious bridge players, on the other hand, "cheat" all the time; the underhanded giving of signals is an extension of normal bidding behavior in which players try to give each other clues as to their holdings.[7]

To return to the question of economic incentives, the pursuit of material acquisition is no different in this respect. In a capitalist society entrepeneurs engaged in successful competitive enterprise behave like Bobby Fischer or Tamerlane—or like a serious rapist. Anyone who expects otherwise is engaged in self-delusion. However, there are all sorts of enterprise, just as there are all sorts of games and all sorts of sexual environments. A publishing house, for example, may be the site of unending (figurative) back-stabbing, throat-cutting, and other behaviors designed to secure the position of editor-in-chief and relegate all other candidates to the dust heap. At the end of the day, though, the winner merely has a six-figure salary instead of five, the power to hire, fire, and generally push around a relatively small staff of underlings, and socially harmless perquisities such as never having to pay for lunch, make coffee, or buy the morning newspaper. The winner's personality may be no different from that of Jay Gould or Commodore Vanderbilt, but there are no financial empires at stake nor financial ruin for anybody. The winner, of course, might also be Rupert Murdoch, winner of a competition not to be a mere editor but to be that much more powerful figure, a publisher. As such he might well be eager to expand his budding communications empire. But if a rigorously enforced antimonopoly law limited his holdings to one newspaper, one television station, one chain of bookstores, etc., then that is all he could seek ruthlessly to obtain: after which, like every past tycoon who could find nowhere else to expand, he would have to start endowing museums and philanthropic foundations.

Thus when a defender of capitalism writes that "democratic capitalists hold that every person of talent—musical, intellectual, economic—should have every opportunity to discover and develop his talents," he has said nothing that (the gender pronoun aside) could not be agreed to by any egalitarian.[8] What is really in question is the extent of the special rewards, if any, *deserved* by "economic talent" and the extent of the special incentives, if any, *required* by it. The first question we have already answered in chapter 1. As to the second, we do not, after all, reward talented musicians or intellectuals with far-reaching rights of ownership over the activities of thousands or millions of other people, nor do we think that the promise of such rewards is necessary to encourage them to develop their talents. The search for mastery is undoubtedly a real human desire; but the promise of unlimited wealth, as far as we can tell, inspires only the search for mastery over the pursuit of wealth itself. In what sense, for example, is the Rockefeller family's control over oil and banking empires, and several governments as well, the kind of "reward" that would-be developers of economic talent require?[9] Remove that kind of excess power and wealth, and budding capitalists, male or female, can be left free to go out and engage in as many capitalist relations as they can find other adults to freely consent to; and they can be paid whatever return their efforts, in the viewpoint of their fellows, deserve.

The crux of the matter here is whether *unlimited greed* as a legitimized, if not dominant, motive to social action is necessary to economic growth. Accumulation for its own sake could not possibly be the primary orientation of a social order based on democratic equality. We have seen what other impulses—to give care where needed, to give mutual respect, to control surplus inequalities and privileges—would have to take precedence over it. Can the drive for accumulation, private or public, survive in a cultural milieu that requires it to be hamstrung? Although we can hardly answer the question with confidence, it is surely the case that around the world innovation in the development of potentially useful goods has often, even most of the time, sprung forth from people who had no expectation at all of becoming titans of industry.[10] Children take up the violin and play it for the rest of their lives, even though they know fairly quickly that they will never be Anne-Sophie Mutter or play with the New York Philharmonic; graduate students decide to be political theorists without the faintest hope that they will ever be featured in the last chapter of a textbook that begins with Plato. If, as Michael Novak implies, "economic talent" belongs to the same species as our other talents, why should we think it is a special case?

In the end, the only interesting reason for reserving special rewards for entrepeneurs has to do not with acquisitiveness but with power. Power over others, it may be argued, is in fact an essential, ineradicable aspect of what we mean by "economic talent." More precisely, it can plausibly be said that whatever the economic stakes, there is no *psychic* reward in being an owner who cannot also be a boss; who cannot make a meaningful business decision without having to honor the wishes of employees, voters, shareholders, and any and all others who consider themselves the boss's democratic equals. If one's special talent is to be able to make such decisions and make them intelligently, why share them with others? A professor of political science doesn't take a vote of the students before requiring them to read *On the Social Contract* (instead of watching *Seinfeld*, say) and probably would go into some other profession if that was the university's rule of behavior. To paraphrase Marx again, a general of industry who has to take a vote of the workers before deciding to expand operations overseas (say), would be like an army general who has to take a vote of the troops before deciding to attack. Who would want to be such a general?

The rhetorical question has a plausible force; that is, it is superficially persuasive. In truth, both analogies are poor. When all is said and done, the reality of military life is that collectively soldiers are cannon fodder, but individually they want to live. That is why large armies always have to be conscripted; there are too few men around willing to subject themselves to that reality voluntarily. Contrarily, students do in fact "vote"—with their feet—all the time. They don't have to take a course that requires reading Rousseau, after all. In short, students have the right of exit, and soldiers don't. If we now think about workers in a capitalist society, what we see is that although they formally have the same right of exit as students, it is often virtually useless to them; they are more like soldiers. (This is the meaning of MacPherson's reply to Friedman, quoted on p. 29 above). The same is true of women, who have the legal right of exit from male domination through divorce but often can't afford to exercise it. Contrarily, if workers in general and women specifically did effectively have the right of exit, in the sense that alternative jobs or a basic income were guaranteed them, then employers would *want* to consult with them and men would *want* to take their rights seriously; no one wants to depend on disgruntled persons who might just walk out at any time.

Part of any talent is making it seem useful or attractive to other people. If I can't get students interested in Rousseau, eventually I will stop assigning his works, or stop teaching political theory altogether. If no one comes to hear Anne-Sophie Mutter, she won't be a solo violinist for long. In the world of goods production, the correlative ground rule of capitalism has been that only the *consumers* of those goods have to be satisfied by an employer of labor, because consumers have the right of exit: they can buy something else (perhaps). This is why Marx declaims sarcastically that the sphere "within whose boundaries the sale and purchase of labour-power goes on, is in fact a very Eden of the innate rights of man." Labor power is only a commodity like any other; the seller doesn't have to sell it and the buyer doesn't have to buy it. They are "equal."[11] However, within the production process, as Marx went on to point out, exploitation does takes place, and the worker can expect "a hiding." If he were free to leave the production process and start his own business, then he would not be subject to exploitation . . . but how many workers can do that? Workers, therefore, do not have to be satisfied by employers because their formal right of exit is ineffectual (until and unless they form unions or political parties that change the rules of the game and achieve some version of the right to strike and be rehired, grievance procedures, approval of layoffs, etc.).

Therefore, assuming some semblance of private property

in means of production (in fact the requirements should be the same for public ownership as well), equality demands that the owners or managers of that property must be able not only to persuade consumers of the value of their product but also and more importantly to persuade workers of the value of their employment. Undoubtedly this requirement would diminish the attractiveness of being an employer or manager in the eyes of many people. Still, there's no reason to believe that the overall supply of potential managers would thereby be diminished. Persuasiveness in "human relations" is a skill too, and one that is enjoyable to exercise. The more authoritarian the powers of management, the less the need for that important human skill. In a different cultural context the people who possess it might prefer managing firms to advertising their products, or selling insurance door-to-door. Even more, if men had to satisfy women the way women learn to satisfy men—that is, by demonstrating qualities other than earning power—again a different kind of personality would be required to rise to "the top."

Authoritative statements about the incentives needed to get this or that done always proceed in the same way, by presuming that the people who wind up doing things in our society are the only people capable of doing those things and that the way we get things done is the only way we are capable of getting them done. The presumptuousness of this kind of thinking suggests one final consideration about the so-called division of labor.

The vaunted efficiency of patriarchalist capitalism inheres partially in its elaboration of the occupational division of labor. In principle there is nothing either unjust or irrational about that division of labor; it rests on the reasonable proposition that not everybody can do everything well, and many people can only do one thing well. Egalitarians do not doubt diversity of accomplishment; they celebrate it. In practice, however, on the one hand an obscene diversity of *reward* for relatively similar human effort *is* unjust and irrational; when "rewards" are appropriated rather than earned, their "contribution" to society becomes negative.[12] And so too, on the other hand, is the relegation of vast numbers of human beings not to "manual" labor, but to a reserve army of *menial* labor from which they can never escape and which needlessly constrains or mutilates human talent. It's the practice not the principle that needs to be changed.

"Some mute inglorious Milton here may rest . . ."

Merely changing practices is not enough, though, as we confront what Marx distinguished as the *social* division of labor, which for the most part doesn't distribute either occupations or efficiency. Instead, the social division of labor distributes power and privilege, conveying a monopoly in planning to a small class of people, mostly male and mostly white, who vigorously police their class and occupational boundaries, excluding everyone else from participation in the decisions that shape the social and natural worlds. This monopoly is rational and efficient only if we believe that the great majority of people and especially of women are incapable of mustering the intelligence and mastering the skills necessary to take responsibility for the productive use of labor-saving techniques and technology. It is not the "natural" distribution of "human capital" but rather particular, powerful, human beings who have established the categories of manager and laborer, expert and layman, as necessarily being synonymous with the few and the many.

The social division of labor imposes a reduction rather than a maximization of the potential amount and variety of human intelligence to be applied to the solution of technical and organizational problems. The old British "Elevens plus" system was the most literal representation of an elite's penchant for reproducing itself in the narrowest possible way, but even in the more democratic United States the structure of opportunity takes on a similar shape. Those who enter the magic kingdom of the supposed intellectual elite have resources poured into them like gold dust down a funnel; everyone else gets the bare bones of a penurious public educational system. The net result is that we concentrate on developing the capacities of a minority to the utmost and neglect the chance to develop the capacities of the majority.

Moreover, whatever virtue higher education might have as an instruction in independent thought and civic virtue, we are not even certain that our huge investment in it gives a positive economic return to society at large. Used mostly as a credentialing device, it keeps many potentially employable, productive, but less educated workers out of the well-paying sector of a segmented labor market: a sector that, even in its glamorous high-tech division, most of the time doesn't practically require anything more than a good high school education or relevant vocational training. As for the workers who wind up in the least-rewarded positions, there is not the faintest evidence that they are uneducable or untrainable. Our collective refusal to educate or train them for better, higher-paying work *and* then to provide that work can be justified by the redistributive costs of such an effort, but not by anything "natural" about either the distribution of talents or the social division of labor.[13]

We have no idea how much undeveloped talent and consequent social productivity is squandered by our reproduction of the social division of labor. Perhaps we receive a hint from a story that came out of Philadelphia, Pennsylvania, twenty years ago. There, in Vaux Middle School, a school with an almost entirely black constituency, a dedicated teacher set up a school chess team, and encouraged students to try out for it. In return for their commitment, he would teach them the rudiments and then the elaborations of chess—a game that more than any other is associated with what the propagandists of IQ call the highest level of intelligence, that is, abstract reasoning. Three years after he began his voluntary (and unpaid) effort, four boys from a Philadelphia high school that no one anywhere else in the nation had ever heard of had gone to the national tournament finals and had become the middle school chess champions of the United States. By 1998 there were not just one but ten national championship trophies sitting in the principal's office at Vaux Middle School. If I had written "basketball" where I wrote "chess," no one reading these pages would have been even momentarily surprised, for every step of the social division of labor, beginning in the very earliest years of pre-schooling, is set up to produce and reproduce black basketball players and white or Asian American mathematicians and physicists (and chess players). Human beings are indeed rational much of the time, if not exactly in the way economists suggest they are. If expectations are unlikely to be fulfilled, then they will be reduced, and the people with those reduced expectations will contribute much less to overall social well-being than they might have otherwise. Conversely, when it seems that raised expectations might be in even the faintest degree realistic, as in the case of those chess-playing young black men, then people's "capabilities" can suddenly, from the skewed perspective of an ignorant outside observer, rise quite astonishingly.

In the end, from watching the development of our children we learn little or nothing about "human nature" and its alleged limits and everything about how we spend our money and what we spend it on. The egalitarian argument is that we are spending the wrong amounts of it on the wrong things. We get what we spend for, and because so much of our inequality is surplus inequality, what we get is potentially much less, in ultimate social value, than what we could have.

6) THE PROBLEM OF COMPENSATION

The Paradox

IF WE LOOK back at the previous discussion, we immediately see that there is a problem inherent in any consideration of equal opportunity. Much of what I've called surplus inequality is explained by the normal operations of the capitalist division of labor. But as the terms "gendered state" and "racial state" suggest, there is a form of surplus inequality—*castelike* inequality—that is not explicable in this way (though as I have noted it makes an excellent labor market rationing device). This is the additional marginalization or exclusion from even the ordinary "technical" division of labor of groups defined as lesser, as inferior. It comprehends the additional discrimination against them that goes on within that division of labor in the form of glass and concrete ceilings; and, even more destructively, in the operation of basic social institutions as well. Women of any skin color or social background are almost everywhere still subject to the presumption that they are a natural servant and sex class, that what they do is not as important as what men do, and that if they're allowed to do what's really important they won't do it as well. On the whole, of course, exactly what it is that women are denied tends to be a function of how they are defined socially in addition to their gender. Being denied consideration for a

CEO position because you're a woman who is incidentally white is not quite the same deviation from equal treatment as being turned away from interviews for secretarial jobs because you're a Latina. But it is equally discriminatory.

Discrimination against minorities because they are minorities is not in any sense more fundamental than discrimination against women as a class; but it is very often even worse. For example, this is the fate of black or Hispanic persons, male or female, in the United States; Irish, black, or Asian residents in England; or the Algerian or Indonesian or Turkish immigrants who have come to stay in France or the Netherlands or Germany. Almost all of these are denied equal employment opportunities on the basis of stereotypes about their behavior; barred from the housing they can afford, which is already less than what is available to their white counterparts; regularly harassed by the police; warehoused in disciplinary and penal institutions (including foster homes) from an early age; deprived (at least in the privatized American health sector) of access to standard health care; excluded from educational tracks that lead to professional careers; and so on and on. In every advanced capitalist nation where they are a serious presence, moreover, a sub-industry of pseudoscience and complicit journalism grows up to prove their "inferiority" (sometimes along with that of women in general), and thus to suggest that their condition is no one's fault but their own and is irremediable. What Marx called "the reserve army of labor," the labor force that depresses average wages both as a threatening mass of the unemployed *and* as the recipients of substandard pay for fractional jobs, takes on the character of a *caste* (or series of castes) as well as that of a class.

Equal opportunity of any kind, weak as well as strong, is subverted by the treatment of women as though they are naturally unfree persons who must be attached to a man and children to realize their innate ends. It is also subverted and often turned violently against itself by the creation of a hypostasized "other" identified by skin color, traditional language, etc. Such "others" are a living reproach to the rhetoric of equal opportunity, and the terror "others" inspire—that equal opportunity may all be a lie after all—breeds further savagery in *their* treatment, whether by the police or by the local version of skinheads. Thus the abolition of discrimination—in the housing market, in the legal and penal systems, at places of work, in the industries that generate and distribute mass cultural images, in medical treatment, in schools and in access to schooling—is more than anything else the sine qua non of equal opportunity.[1]

That abolition can be accomplished in part by compensatory programs of education and training, starting at the earliest possible age, for those who would otherwise remain undertrained. But since their objective lack of preparation is only the beginning of their problems, the provision of fair opportunity also, again, requires regulatory state agencies with coercive powers. These are necessary effectively to prohibit the destructive discriminations that are faced not only by the undereducated but often even by members of minority groups and women in general, who confront a discriminatory civil society despite having faithfully followed all the conventional paths to self-betterment.

This conclusion—that some form of administrative enforcement of law is necessary—does not come from any romantically elitist notion that public bureaucrats are better persons than private employers or that mass political parties can somehow make a silk purse of liberal governance and toleration out of a sow's ear of bigoted public opinion. Rather, the justification of coercive protection for the excluded and marginalized—of antidiscrimination *law*—lies in the peculiar result of combining social psychological perceptions with individual calculations of utility. If I know that others are discriminating, and if discrimination seems on the surface to be an effective rationing device, and if I therefore have nothing obvious to gain personally (except a sense of moral righteousness) by refusing to discriminate, the odds that I will join the discriminating crowd rise dramatically. Just as taxation systems are necessarily obligatory rather than voluntary (because who wants to be the only one paying?), so too are antidiscrimination institutions. And we entrust that necessary work to public law and public employees not because the latter are more noble-spirited persons but because they are more likely to perform faithfully a task that they are being paid to perform as their particular responsibility, and because they have nothing to lose by and no conflict of interest in so doing.

If we try to sum up everything that has been said so far, what we see is that equality defined simply as equal opportunity begins in the classic stance of early modern liberal thinkers. Its familiar components are careers open to the talents; no privileges of birth; the law to treat every law-abiding person according to the same standards. Attempts to realize the promise of that philosophical stance, though, gradually but inevitably move in another direction. That direction led Mill to subscribe to the International Workingman's Association and support an early version of the welfare state; it led John Dewey toward a theory of participatory democracy; and it led Franklin Delano Roosevelt to proclaim that "a civilization is measured not by how much it gives to those who already have a lot, but by how much it gives to those who have little." There is not only a distinction between formal, legal equal opportunity, and strong equal opportunity, but there is also this inevitable connection between them. The boundary that divides them is permeable and shifting; the notion that they represent opposed principles is false. Recognizing that falsity is crucial to an understanding of race and gender politics in the United States today.

The issue that more than any other unites the two conceptions of equality is the issue of compensation. That is, what is to be done about those groups of people who (as the case may be) have been subject to so many oppressions and deprivations in the past, that the existence of "a level playing field" in the present legitimately seems like a mockery to them? What are we to do when enforcing the abolition of discrimination seems to demand positive, *affirmative* action by agents of public law enforcement to make certain that the premises of past, legalized, discrimination still do not undergird contemporary practices?

Let us consider the following parable: Major State U., an all-white public university, is playing Deltaville College, a small all-black college. At the end of the first half the score is 54–0 State, a margin dictated not only by the fact that State is a much bigger institution, but by the much more salient fact that State has played the entire first half with fourteen men on the field, its reasoning being that Negroes are "inferior" persons and should not be allowed to play against whites on equal terms; indeed, they should feel privileged to be playing with them at all. At halftime, however, Deltaville secures an injunction from a judge, who holds that the game has been unfair: "Football," he declares, "is a color-blind game, meant to be played with eleven players on a side, neither more nor less." On being told of this decision, State's coach graciously accepts it and says, "let's go out there and play the game." "Wait a minute," Deltaville's coach replies angrily, "you should play the second half with *eight* men; that's only fair." State's coach then concludes the brief discussion by declaiming authoritatively, "You heard what the judge said; football's supposed to be played with eleven players, otherwise it's unfair. And it's a color-blind game, you don't get three extra players just because you're black. Stop your whining, and get out there and play the game. You're only eight touchdowns behind!"

My mythical game began, of course, under a regime of segregation; that is, under a formally racial state. It is certainly unarguable that in *any* sense of the term "equal opportunity," the first and absolutely essential step in realizing it is permanent abolition of the racial state (and the gender state, and the class state). But this means, surely, not merely that the formally anti-egalitarian institutions of the past must be abolished but that the long-term conditions of inequality they directly created must also be overturned. Otherwise, what is the point of a supposed reform the effects of which are limited to pieces of paper, limited to, as in my parable, useless attempts to rectify an already decisive imbalance? The suburbanization of America, to take one notorious (and very unimaginary) example, proceeded by way of massive housing and transportation subsidies to a middle- and working-class population that was almost entirely white. If it was not white, it was walled into the cities from which it wanted to escape by informal and sometimes formal practices of housing segregation; practices that were fixed firmly in place by the activities (e.g., bias in the underwriting of mortgage, "redlining") both of private banks and real estate agencies and of the very public Home Owners' Loan Corporation and Federal Housing Administration.[2] This process went on for several decades after the end of World War II; it was accompanied by programs of "urban renewal" that often had the effect of demolishing the very urban neighborhoods from which black people were trying to escape, but which remained their only communal recourse as the "white noose" of the suburbs tightened.[3]

This movement was made possible only and entirely by programs of what is nowadays called "government intervention." A half century later, attempts to rectify its destructive effects (such as urban public housing programs) are being eliminated, or mostly have been eliminated, in the name of "getting government off our backs." But of course government has now been "on the backs" of the same people twice: once to reward those who would keep them segregated, and a second time to prevent them from ameliorating the consequences of that enforced segregation.

The paradox of neutral state institutions—institutions that supposedly leave careers open to the talents and lives open to voluntary choice—is thereby revealed. At first their vaunted neutrality is a sham; when the sham is finally exposed, the response of those who benefited from the sham is to say that now it's time for the state to be *really* neutral, for the market to be *really* "free." To do nothing is proclaimed to be preferable than to undo what has already, fatefully, been done. An activist policy with a very deadly core is replaced by a laissez-faire policy with no core at all: what Senator Moynihan once called "benign neglect."

This historical movement reaches its ineluctable climax when, finally, urban segregation produces its promised outcome. This is, on the one hand, a class of people, locked into those decaying parts of the cities that received neither urban renewing nor suburbanizing subsidies, who are mostly poor, mostly nonwhite (as that is socially defined), and suffer disproportionately from every maladjustment, dysfunctional condition, and daily oppression known to affluent modern societies.[4] On the other hand, those who do succeed in escaping the conditions of this figurative ghetto, always one step (and several subsidies) behind the white Americans who were the main beneficiaries of public policy, come to form a superficially successful middle class. Even it, however, always trails after itself the visible reminders of second-class citizenship that link it back to the stigmatized ghetto.

To be white in the United States is just to be a person; to be black in the United States is to be black. Seven black (or Hispanic or Asian) students eating with each other in a dining commons are being "tribal" (as Jews used to be "clannish") or "huddling together"; the forty white students in the room are just having dinner. No journalist writing a news story ever makes certain to let the readers know that Trent Lott is white or, conversely, ever forgoes letting the readers know that Carol Moseley-Braun is black. She, as everyone knows, is the first black female Senator in American history. Imagine if every news story about the Senate's majority leader were to begin, "Trent Lott, the seventy-fourth white male senator from Mississippi . . ." The polity, in other words, remains a racial polity (and a gendered polity, as indicated by the fact that any informed person, on being asked how many male senators there were, would count up the females and then subtract from one hundred), just as social policies remain racial policies and the rigorous, neutral enforcement of "the law" ensures that it remains a racial law.

To understand this connection is to understand the public policy of race, much of the public policy of gender, and specifically the public policy of the contemporary lightning rod for critics of egalitarianism, affirmative action. The problem is a historical one, and at first glance it seems insoluble. We begin with a classical liberal tradition that seems to reject any kind of recognition of persons by the law. On reflection, what is most noteworthy about this tradition is not its so-called affinity for laissez-faire economics. None of the great Anglo-Saxon liberals opposed appropriate public remedies for "privately" contrived injustices. Even Jeremy Bentham, who fought to abolish the poor laws in Britain, did so because at that time social utility demanded, or seemed to demand, a free market in labor, not because he thought government intervention was wrong as a matter of principle.

However, the bedrock demand of classical liberalism has always been for equal treatment before the law; and what that really means was, again, stated best by Rousseau: "the general will, to be truly such, should be general in its object as well as in its essence; that it should come from all to apply to all; *and that it loses its natural rectitude when it is directed toward any individual, determinate object.*"[5] Rousseau idiosyncratically meant by the general will laws produced by the people themselves meeting in assembly rather than by representatives. But his insight works just as well applied to any legitimate lawmaking process, such as contemporary versions of representative government.

The kind of equalization we are considering here, because it is trying to undo what has been done to a specific group of people, as opposed to simply redistributing income via a progressive income or wealth tax, seems indeed to be "directed toward" a "determinate object." The policies that it generates can then be said, with some plausibility, to have lost their "natural rectitude"; to take away from this person and give to that one. They have apparently become, not only by Rousseau's standard but by almost any familiar standard, unjust.

The critique of affirmative action that follows on this analysis is therefore invariably constructed around the phrase I've already quoted, one of the most famous epigrams in American constitutional history. In Justice John Marshall Harlan's words, from his dissent in the 1896 case of *Plessy v. Ferguson*: "Our Constitution is colorblind . . . it neither knows nor tolerates classes among citizens." And, a few sentences earlier, "In respect of civil rights, common to all citizens, the Constitution of the United States does not, I think, permit any public authority to know the race of those entitled to be protected in the enjoyment of such rights."[6] An epigram, however, is not a theory, let alone a principle. Before leaping to any conclusions based on that epigram, we want to make certain that we understand it in its intended context.

The most important point to remember about Harlan's dictum is that it occurred in a context of legalized segregation, not of favoritism toward a class of people thought to be in need of a helping hand. *Plessy v. Ferguson* was a case in which the Supreme Court majority upheld a Jim Crow statute that made it a *crime* "for a citizen of either race to enter a coach that has been assigned to citizens of the other race." The "color blindness" of the Constitution means, as Harlan said, that the law cannot discriminate in that way. To return to Rousseau's language, its stated purposes can only be general, never determinate. "Color blindness" (or any similar kind of "blindness"), is thus the bedrock principle of equal opportunity in the traditional sense; of nondiscrimination. If you or I get, or fail to get, where we are trying to go, we do it or don't do on our own effort, not because any "public authority" has labeled us as belonging to a certain class and then forbidden members of that class to go wherever it is we are trying to go.

How, though, is this "color-blind" Constitution to be applied when there actually *are* classes of the kind that it supposedly neither "knows nor tolerates"? A state university, we assume, may not have separate admissions procedures or quotas for "whites" and "blacks," for it should not even know (in a formal legal sense) whether its applicants are white or black. But here the problem arises, and the paradox of "neutrality" asserts itself. The university does know the race of its applicants, and it can't help but know. And perhaps it really does informally discriminate against those who are black (or Jewish, or female, or of Asian origin). This of course was true in most of American higher education at least until the 1950s, when the Supreme Court in the series of cases leading up to *Brown v. Board of Education* forbade racial segregation or discrimination in institutions of higher education. But suppose now, fifty years later, the percentage of one of these "classes" in a given institution (e.g., blacks) is no higher than it was in 1947 when discrimination was being officially practiced? Perhaps the Constitution, through "the public authorities," is knowing and tolerating classes after all? Perhaps the authorities are still discriminating, though now more discreetly.

"Affirmative action" is designed to make certain that this is not happening; to make the promise of *traditional equal opportunity* come true. We will never understand the peculiar practices that have grown up around it if we persist in thinking that affirmative action is some exotic postliberal (or illiberal) plant nurtured in a radical egalitarian hothouse. Rather, it is intended to be classical liberalism in effective action; its announced goal is not to overturn "merit," as has been claimed by its opponents, but to make the betrayed promise of "merit" come true.

Why then am I, as an administrator of some public or private institution of any kind, compelled to take "affirmative" steps to recruit and admit or hire certain kinds of persons? Why, as is so often the case, do I even voluntarily adopt a program that compels me to do what presumably I want to do anyway (or else why would I be trying to force myself to do it)? The answer is that I know I have discriminated in the past, and I suspect that I am likely to go on doing so in the present and future, *despite my own contrary intention*. Because I am, say, a white American, or a white American male, or just a male (depending on whose rights are at stake), I do not trust myself, nor can I expect to be trusted by others. Therefore I recognize (or, if I don't, the state recognizes) that my behavior needs to be monitored for some (unspecified) length of time, until and unless I (and this means not just myself but all representative persons in my kind of position) have demonstrated that the impulse to discriminate has disappeared.[7] Nor will it do to say, as the critics of affirmative action persist in saying, that whatever problems have existed in the past no longer exist, since more and more minorities are admitted to first-class colleges and universities and so many women are being admitted to graduate schools. These changes have all occurred during the period in which affirmative action has been mandated, and to suggest that they have occurred not because of but in spite of affirmative action is to twist common sense out of any reasonable shape. It is as though one were to say, to speak of a different (but analogous) form of compensatory assistance, that the willingness of men to make alimony payments shows that the legal enforcement of alimony awards is no longer necessary; or that so-called deadbeat dad laws are no longer needed because fathers are now being forthcoming with their child support payments. Worse yet, of course, the critic who argues against affirmative action from the alleged lack of its necessity has already surrendered any argument against it from principle. Once the discussion is made to turn on a point of fact, we will do much better (as is always the case) to pay attention to what is actually happening in people's lives—denials of tenure to women at institutions of higher education, discrimination against women and minorities in hiring and promotion at major corporations and public agencies—rather than to aggregated statistics about abstract levels of group success or failure. The officials who force coercive systems of fair procedure on themselves may know exactly what they are doing.

Now we can see that "color blindness" (or, as we shall see, "gender blindness") is not as obvious a stance as the opponents of affirmative action have made it out to be. Let us think back to *Plessy v. Ferguson* and the segregation of public transport, for example. In 1954, when I climb onto a bus in Tennessee, I find that every apparently black person on that bus is sitting in a rear seat and all the front seats are taken by apparently white persons. If (as once happened to me) I retreat to the back of the bus to find a vacant seat, I discover that the bus will not move until I have returned to the front: better to stand as a white than to sit as a black.

Imagine now that I repeat my trip fifteen or twenty years later, well after the Civil Rights Act has struck down the laws that made the bus driver's behavior not only possible, but mandatory. But let us also suppose now, as a fantasy (perhaps), that traveling through the South once again, I were to find that every time I get on a bus all the blacks are still sitting in the back, and the whites up front; and that when I expostulate about this I get hostile and threatening looks from the whites and fearful warning gestures from the blacks. I call a policeman, who looks the situation over and assures me that the seating pattern is perfectly voluntary. It just so happens that black people like to sit in the rear, and no well-intentioned law can budge them from that preference.

If he were a lawyer instead of a policeman, he might say, "The Constitution is color-blind, and therefore the laws are color-blind too, now that the Civil Rights Act has been passed. Since the Constitution and the laws are color-blind, we have to assume that people are just sitting where they want to sit as a matter of their free choice. And you can't ask me to move some of the black people up front and the white people to the rear, because I represent the law and as such I neither know nor tolerate classes." To which, to conclude this second parable, I might reply, "It may be true that you don't officially 'know' classes, but you officially *are* tolerating them."

This particular version of tacit or de facto segregation does not (one hopes) now exist as starkly as I've imagined it. But it does exist in housing, in employment, and in education, and even in the provision of public transportation (which rarely serves the poorest quarters of any city with any adequacy). And wherever we do encounter it we will also inevitably encounter the rationalization that it just reflects what people "really" want; or that it just reflects the way resources or talent are "really" distributed. No one is doing anything; things just happen that way.

So the issue of principle confronting affirmative action—the requirement of "color blindness"—is not nearly as clear cut as it seems. That is also true of the subsidiary ground on which affirmative action is often attacked, the ground of social utility; or rather, as we've seen earlier, social utility masquerading as "merit."

In the words of Thomas Sowell, a leading opponent of affirmative action, "The problem is not how you will motivate a very tiny number of people who are currently eligible for these programs. The problem is, how are you going to increase that pool of eligible people?"[8] "Eligible" here is meant to suggest that criteria of "merit" are at stake, but in fact the number of people admitted to any position in the overall division of labor is quite obviously a matter of nothing but social utility. In this perspective, the real problem of "eligibility" is that if the same kinds of people who once told Americans that black people "really" wanted segregation are now telling us what black people "really" are "eligible" for, then the socalled color blindness of the law is only superficial.[9] What critics of affirmative action like Thomas Sowell cannot acknowledge (for to acknowledge it would be to cast doubt on his own social position as a trained "expert") is that changes in the division of labor would produce concomitant changes in the determination of whose talents we (that is, the body politic as a whole) want to put to use.[10]

Devote the entire military budget, except for the maintenance and supply of ground forces, to improving public education in the cities (a quite reasonable proposition from a socially utilitarian standpoint), and we would *ipso facto* turn up an immense number of previously unheard-of black persons "eligible" to be schoolteachers. Thus the only thing we ultimately accomplish by invoking the spirit of Justice Harlan, is to reemphasize that we must look beneath the formal legal surface when we ask the question "who is really capable of doing what?"

A well-known, mean-spirited reply to that question goes something as follows: "How would you like to have brain surgery performed on you by a beneficiary of affirmative action?" Why the most notoriously hierarchical occupational division of labor should suddenly fail to be enforced (neurosurgery being surely one of the most exclusive and rewarding specialties in any field, with no one getting to enter it simply by virtue of having been admitted to medical school) is never explained by the authors of such questions.

But again, the issue as raised gives us the opportunity directly to confront the question of social utility, and confronting it in this context again helps us to understand the distinction between the formal and the real.

Although an anecdote is not a theory, an anecdote may be helpful here. Some years ago, before the era of gender integration, I taught briefly at Haverford College, then considered one of the two or three best colleges for men in the United States. Appalled by one upper-class student's midterm exam performance, I went to the appropriate campus office to look up his record in order to discover how a functionally illiterate ignoramus had been admitted to such an elite institution. The dossier was revealing. To begin with, the young man was a football player and a pre-med major. But he was hardly the kind of student who'd always been a whiz at the hard sciences while being unable to handle the vagueness of social studies. On the contrary, he'd never been a whiz at anything, not even in high school. Clipped to his admissions materials, which unsurprisingly described a multigenerational Haverfordian legacy, was a handwritten note from whoever had interviewed him. It read, in its entirety, "A good all-around lad, should have no trouble finishing in the bottom quarter of his class."

Aside from its curious wording—this "lad" would have had "trouble" finishing anything but dead last, and in any event one fourth of any group will always have "no trouble" finishing in its bottom quarter—the note perfectly described several "pre-med" young men I had encountered some years earlier while traveling to Europe by ocean liner. They were on their way to a second-rate Swiss or Belgian medical school, from which they would indubitably return to practice surgery, although probably not of the neuro- variety. Perhaps because it's often claimed that surgery requires physical strength, many surgeons look, as did the young lad, like offensive guards from a mediocre college football team. (I've never met a general practitioner in "family practice" who could be so described.) I have no idea whether my shipmates or my student became competent or incompetent surgeons, but I am pretty certain that investigation would turn up no correlation between their class rank and any particular outcome.

Thus, to move from the anecdotal to the general, the most well-known study of inequality in the United States concludes that academic ability positively effects "earnings," with each fifteen points difference in "test scores" predicting a 17 percent difference in earnings. But the authors of the study did not consider earnings in any way a proxy for merit, and they also pointed out that "the effects of test performance on earnings are not very large relative to the overall earnings gap between the rich and the poor in general. The best paid fifth of male earners earns about five times what the worst paid fifth earn, and the disparity is even greater if one compares, say, the top and bottom tenths. Our findings therefore, do not characterize the United States as a "meritocracy," at least if merit is measured by general cognitive skills."[11]

My former student is almost certainly by now in the top fifth, and probably in the top tenth. I doubt if he can yet write a coherent paragraph about anything. All of this is only guesswork, of course, and even less than anecdotes do guesses prove anything. But the hard fact is that in those days the bottom quarter of the graduating class at Haverford (and like institutions) was composed entirely of white "lads." (The black students would have been mostly Nigerian soccer players, plus a handful of "African Americans" who would have to have been exceptional students to be admitted to elite institutions.) No one then ever asked whether we would like to have surgery performed on us by, or bridges built by, or money invested by, such a suspect character as someone who'd finished in the bottom quarter of his class. *Only* when affirmative action insured that many students fitting that description would be nonwhite did various persons suddenly find it useful to raise the question of social utility. As with Carol Moseley-Braun, in a racial state, even after it has been formally deracialized, it is still the minority race that is always at issue; as with Trent Lott, "whiteness" is simply the way things normally are.

In short, neither political principles of state neutrality nor utilitarian considerations about social "needs" provides a definitive grasp on the rightness (or wrongness) of "affirmative action" in the search for equal opportunity.

Neutral Justice and Equal Opportunity

So in specific circumstances of past deprivation, some of which may still obtain in the United States, it is not unjust, not without natural rectitude, to provide a remedy that directly redresses, or compensates, the victims of that deprivation. But what about the much greater difficulty, the prospect that in justly compensating those who lack some good they ought to have, we will unjustly take away from others who have more of that good but have attained it guiltlessly or who are even have-nots themselves?

The conflict between neutral justice and equality, if there is such a conflict, is not that we will compensate those who don't deserve compensation, for any society we know of has always incorporated precisely such a moral order. The conflict, rather, is that (we fear) compensation of some may be taken to require the deprivation of others; others whose social identity is given, at least negatively, by the terms of the compensatory legislation (e.g., white males), and whose deprivation demonstrates the law's lack of "natural rectitude."

However, how we are to view this supposed conflict is dependent on the context within which it occurs, and in fact there are several differing contexts within which the protean term "affirmative action" has to be considered, before we can make sense of its meaning and the arguments about it. Although the term is usually taken as applying to admissions procedures in higher education (as well as "set-asides" in government contracting), the process it designates also applies, if usually only informally, to appointments to policy-making positions; and to recruitment and promotion in public and private bureaucracies. The filling of administrative and managerial positions within a private firm (personnel officer, vice president for sales, etc.), a public bureaucracy (regional director of an agency, school administrator), or the social order as a whole (judge, cabinet member, legislator) call upon exactly the same considerations— dealing with both the legacy of past discrimination and its continuing presence—as do its more familiar uses.

Thus, although not always recognized, the role of affirmative action in public life is clear cut and unambiguous, as the following example demonstrates. A woman, Judge S., who is now a judge on a federal appeals court, tells this story about her appointment. Then president Carter had instituted a series of screening commissions (the first president to do so) and had enjoined them to discover more female and minority candidates for the federal courts. Judge S. was a well-reputed district court judge in the circuit from which she, along with one other woman, was recommended for a higher appointment. The screening panel for that circuit was headed by a male judge from the same circuit and had one female member. As the panel began its business, the chairman announced a new procedure, designed to "shorten the process": each member would be able to blackball one candidate. He then began the panel's deliberations by blackballing Judge S. Appalled, the panel's lone female member asked him how he could possibly justify this action. "Well," he replied politely, "she has four children; she couldn't possibly undertake the workload of an appellate judge for a circuit covering so many states." Unable to think of anything to say to that, she fell silent; and the blackballing proceeded around the table. When it came to her, she proceeded to throw out the name of another distinguished (male) judge from that circuit, who was known to be the chairman's favorite candidate. Another appalled silence; then, "what could possibly be the grounds for that?" he asked her. "Well," she replied, "he has five children; how could he possibly do the work?" After a moment, the chairman announced that perhaps the new procedure was a bad idea; why didn't they start all over, without blackballing? Judge S. was recommended to the president, and has had a distinguished judicial career since.

In 1991 then president Bush, without benefit of screening commissions, nominated Judge Clarence Thomas to the Supreme Court, with the encomium that he was "the most qualified person for the job." As compared with the nomination of Judge S., this was a palpable lie, with reference to a man who had served as a judge for only one year, and whose previous career was distinguished mostly by his political correctness while serving the Republican Party. What Justice Thomas had, of course, was ideological acceptability. He was the perfect candidate for a president who, like his predecessor Ronald Reagan, had appointed almost no minority candidates to the federal court system. Unlike those many other sitting black judges whose résumés suggested much greater qualifications and capability, he was a black judge whose conservatism was absolutely unimpeachable. What is interesting about Justice Thomas's story is not the question of his qualifications; there have been many purely political appointees to the Court and at least one of them, Hugo Black, became one of its greatest members. What is interesting, rather, is that no opponent of affirmative action, and especially no black opponent of affirmative action, such as Ward Connerly or Thomas Sowell, had the faintest negative word to say about one of the crassest expressions of "affirmative action" on record.

Taken together, the two stories reveal much about the concepts of "reverse discrimination" and "preference" and the false consciousness that surrounds them. Both Judge S. and Justice Thomas (until he revealed himself to be a liar under oath) were "qualified" for the positions to which they were being nominated. Whether either or both of them was "most qualified" is unknowable and irrelevant; the phrase is sheer cant. Moreover, the presence of ideological preference in this particular appointment process is not only expectable but reasonable. The president (Carter or Bush) was elected (by a majority in both cases) presumably on the basis of his ideology (among other factors, but probably the primary factor). Why shouldn't he name judges whose views he finds sympathetic? Judges are not apolitical persons, they have to have views on the issues, and why not the views of the leader who was elected to do a job which includes naming them?

In this context, in other words, the question of "qualifications" is almost always inappropriate in the form that public discussion usually gives it. There are some public decision-making positions, but very few, for which we actually rank candidates hierarchically. Most of the time we group them into *pools* of the qualified and appoint, select, or admit from within those pools. As anyone who has ever participated in a departmental search for an academic appointment knows, "self-serving nonsense" is the kindest description of the proposition that such searches actually proceed via a narrowing-down process that results in the selection of "the best"; even among those who suppose themselves to be the most dedicated to "quality." (If any academic reader doubts this, a good exercise would be to make up an "objective," quantifiable scale pertaining to the various desiderata—and there are many—of a particular position that was the subject of a recent search, apply it to all the candidates retrospectively, and then try to make the actual outcome of the search conform to the results of the scaling process without deliberately cooking the books. It cannot be done.)

The best candidate is simply the one who turned out to be most desirable to the people doing the hiring or admitting. Or, if scoring the highest on some credentialing test, the best candidate is often simply the one who turned out to be most desirable to the people making up the test in the first place. Most credentialing tests, in fact, are used by public (less often private) bureaucracies, and their purpose is primarily to avoid accusations of favoritism. The beauty of an "objective" test is not that it predicts performance but that it takes the ultimate decision out of the hands of any identifiable and potentially reproachable human being. As a justification, "he scored highest on the qualifying exam" has more in common with "the dog ate my homework" than it has with "he was clearly the most qualified person for this very important job." It is an excuse, not an explanation.

A corollary to this point is that, "best" or not, no one is

owed any particular public position. Given a list of a hundred qualified judges to be considered for promotion to a higher level of the judiciary, it would be perfectly reasonable *and fair* to promote any one of them over the others. Moreover, there is a good reason to assert that if *all* appointments to judicial or supervisory administrative positions at any level of government for, say, the next twenty years, were to be made solely from lists containing female and minority candidates, it would still be too little. When "the law" is authoritatively interpreted and enforced, it ought to be interpreted and enforced by people who are likely to recognize rather than deny its built-in discriminations, ambiguities, and favoritisms.

In the United States, acknowledged and unacknowledged discrimination and favoritism have been *the* single most decisive factor in the history of "democratic" public life. Women from all social backgrounds have been excluded because they have been thought to be unfit or "not tough enough" for decision-making responsibilities. The gendered state as well as the gendered corporation are literally gendered, that is, masculinized; the "state based on force," as Max Weber called it, is a state based on (heterosexual) men, or women who can imitate men ("G.I. Jane").[12] The racialization of the state, even three decades after the passage of the Civil Rights Act of 1964, remains a profound determinant of the visible face of authority.

The vengefulness of a Right that has been attempting to overthrow a legitimately elected president since the day of his first election, together with the institutionalized ignorance, depoliticization, and prurience of the mass media, have obscured what may some day be seen as one of President Clinton's most enduring legacies: the first genuine attempt by any American leader to change that visible face even slightly. (It's typical that the critics of affirmative action give him no credit for making appointments that they ought to greet as a vindication of their optimism.) Men and women of (especially) African American or Hispanic American (and Native American and to some extent Asian American) background have been excluded simply because they are outsiders, if not outcasts. Since the passage of the Civil Rights Act, one public agency after another, federal or state or local, has had to settle class action lawsuits brought by female or minority employees who have been passed over either in hiring or promotion processes. The powerful appoint or select those whom they know or feel comfortable with; and white men mostly know and feel comfortable with each other.

Two take just three out of hundreds of instances: On February 7, 1998, the Justice Department filed suit against a Dallas suburb for discriminating against minorities in hiring for the police and fire departments. This was not just a case of using an allegedly inappropriate written examination but also of tolerating harassment of nonwhites who did secure employment. Three weeks later, a class action complaint was filed against the Federal Reserve Bank of Chicago for systematic discrimination against blacks over a thirty-year period (roughly the same length of time as the Civil Rights Act had been in force!), as well as a sex discrimination complaint. A few weeks after that, a federal judge instructed the Connecticut suburb of East Haven to come up with remedies for a long history of apparent discrimination in appointments to public service jobs. Never a month goes by, and usually more frequently than that, without a similar complaint being filed somewhere.

This kind of implicit (not to mention explicit) discrimination is not just a formal violation of liberal democratic principles (at least if practiced by publicly funded institutions); it has serious social consequences as well. There is no set of objectively good or fair policies and decisions. There are only those policies and decisions that people "like us" (whoever we are) find familiar and satisfying; and, using our power or authority, we have placed these on the agenda of public life to begin with. In the simplest utilitarian sense, diversity in public life maximizes social utility, for it broadens the range of experiences that are brought to that life.[13] Most especially, in Mill's words, "in the absence of its natural defenders, the interest of the excluded is always in danger of being overlooked; and, when looked at, is seen with very different eyes from those of the persons whom it directly concerns."[14] Whatever diversity is possible in a particular environment (much more in the United States than in Finland, for example), in its absence we know that the rhetoric of equal opportunity remains merely rhetorical.

With respect to private bureaucracies, the situation is somewhat similar. Even though the democratic notion of diverse representation obviously does not apply as strongly, the antidiscrimination principle is still appropriate, and violations of it have been much more prevalent and even more gross (think of Texaco). Is there anyone in the world who believes that banks, insurance companies, and industrial corporations have regularly and diligently hired and promoted "the most qualified" candidates for managerial or service positions? This is another rhetorical question that is again answered by the simple historical fact that in the past two decades almost every major firm in the United States has, like so many public agencies, also had to settle an expensive class action lawsuit.[15] Affirmative action for white men has been the history of private white-collar employment in the United States (and certainly everywhere else).

Whether or to what extent that is still true is a factual question, of course. But with less than three decades' experience of mandated equal employment practices, it would be absurdly premature to dismantle, at a minimum, the institutions of formal search and promotion procedures and the public agencies that oversee them. What I have called the paradox of color blindness simply does not exist in these arenas, for color blindness itself, and gender blindness as well, are still honored mostly in the breach.

Affirmative Action and Higher Education

Since that conclusion is hard to deny, in this realm of employment and promotion the major objection that has been made to affirmative action is to the "red tape" and "paperwork" that accompanies administrative and judicial oversight. It is hard to see, however, how that outcome can be avoided, in that the realistic alternative is a system of hiring quotas that would be considerably more intrusive; nor is it possible to defend oneself against antidiscrimination lawsuits without a paper trail to establish adherence to fair procedures.

Although there has also been much complaint about "set asides" for small business subsidies or contracts, however, the major source of complaint about affirmative action occurs in the realm of higher education.[16] And it is here the apparent paradox of "color blindness" really does reveal itself in starkest relief.

There are two, and only two, considerations for institutions, such as institutions of higher education, making decisions of "admit" or "reject" among a plethora of candidates for admission. The first rule is simply that the principle of nondiscrimination must be obeyed. Or rather, it must be obeyed if the minimal claim of providing formal, legal "equal opportunity" is to have credence. The second rule, however, often contradicts the first, and it is this contradiction that causes a good deal of the confusion and anger over "affirmative action." The second rule is that selection procedures (or procedures of any kind) must faithfully adhere to announced rules of preference.

If a college or university lets it be known that 1100 is the minimum combined SAT score for admission, and then admits minority candidates with combined scores of 1000, it has violated its own rules and thereby betrayed the good-faith expectations of all those applicants (some of whom will now be denied an admission they would otherwise have been granted) whose score was above the supposed minimum. Worse yet, the institution in question will also have failed to follow the first rule, that of nondiscrimination. The rule of nondiscrimination is promulgated precisely to make certain that qualified persons are not turned away, but in this exemplary (and in practice very common) case admission has been granted to candidates who by the institution's own definition are "not equally qualified." The conflict between neutral justice and equality, referred to above, now seems to be unavoidable.

On the face of it, implicit discrimination in higher (and professional graduate) education plays a quite different role than it does in the public and private bureaucracies discussed above. There, so-called tests are most often transparent rationales for hiring the same kind of people one is used to hiring; the employers are not committed to "merit" in any real sense, and often they do indeed intend to discriminate. Most of the time nowadays, however, discrimination in higher education is seemingly accidental, the result of a reliance on criteria that do at least seem to predict performance in school itself with some reliability. Much of the time boards of admission seem to be honestly trying not to discriminate, but believe with equal honesty in test and grade credentials that are distributed one-sidedly. How is this conflict to be resolved?

As the above discussion suggests, the real problem is not who gets admitted, but how "qualified" is defined in the first place. Herein lies the general failure of much public discourse about affirmative action. The real problem is not that unqualified persons have been admitted to, and qualified ones turned away from, institutions of higher education, but that (many of) these institutions have adopted, or have seemed to have adopted, a meretricious standard for admission. In tying their behavior to "objective" test scores and *then* deciding to grant compensatory preference to candidates who don't measure up by that criterion, they are like a man trying to ride on two horses that are charging away in opposite directions. If "aptitude" tests were simply abolished, a major part of the affirmative action discussion would concomitantly disappear.

This is not merely an idle point; it is the heart of the matter. There are practical reasons for not abolishing testing—as for example a resort of last instance, when other rationing devices have failed to prescribe a result for candidate selectors. It is also sometimes the case that "objective test scores" *are* the best way of overcoming genuine prejudice—at least the high scorers from among the stigmatized groups can overcome their stigma. There are no good theoretical reasons for relying on tests, however. Indeed, there are no good theoretical reasons for not conducting college and possibly even graduate school admissions by lottery, and then letting the chips fall where they may—flunking out those who can't do the work, and then helping them to find other avenues of opportunity.

In the more bureaucratized higher education systems of Europe this would be quite possible, and something like it occurs in some nations. On the other hand, given the unique histories, and consequently expectations, of most American colleges and universities, that would be an impossible path to follow; if nothing else, faculties would rebel at the prospect of teaching the intellectually diverse student bodies (and classes) that would ensue. Therefore, either abolishing testing, or seriously reining in its authority, remains the best way to open up American higher education to otherwise excluded groups as well as to improve the experience of that education for most people by making it more socially and intellectually challenging.

The best way to understand aptitude testing, beyond understanding its political usefulness, is as a form of fetishism; that is, the attribution of magical powers to an ordinary phenomenon. In this case the fetishism is the fetishism of numbers, which attributes a concrete reality to mere numbers and then substitutes that for the reality of people's lives. Ward Connerly, Thomas Sowell, et al are fetishists. It would be an ad hominem attack to speculate on the motivations of their fetishism but perfectly justifiable to diagnose it. With respect both to what tests measure, and what those measurements might mean, almost everything important about those lives—and therefore *inter alia* people's real as opposed to paper "qualifications"—remains concealed.

Thus the interpretation of objective tests ignores first, the person's entire prehistory (health, nutrition, sleep, peer group pressures, parental encouragement, etc.), and second, the development of test-taking as a skill. Test-taking is a very particular and specialized way of displaying mental understanding, requiring not just that skill but also an at least intuitive understanding of the social role of the test; and above all a commitment to test taking, a belief (really a magical belief in its own right) in its useful properties. That is, whether the test taker shares the fetishism of testing or at least accepts it as a useful enterprise is central to the ability to take the tests. In addition, the interpretation of tests, unless modified by other considerations, ignores the prior social history of those taking the tests—what social role their kin and peers have typically filled and the kinds of expectations this had bred about displays of intellectual ability. None of these is innate in any sense; all are determined by experience.

As to what objective tests measure, the true answer is, almost nothing of importance. They do not, in the first instance, measure any kind of mental ability that is not defined as such by the self-serving makers and interpreters of the tests, in other words, abilities that are not the same as those they themselves specialize in.[17] What do the tests actually measure then? *They measure what they measure, and nothing else.* We should call it "performative reasoning with printed matter." The key word is "performative"—test-taking is a *performance, a demonstration of ability, not an expression of ability*. And it is performative in the milieu of *print* only.

This is what the testers are interested in, but it has nothing necessary to do with the person's ability to make useful contributions to the world. Above all, tests do not measure a person's *capacity to learn.* They measure learning capability *so far,* as educated (in the United States) by one of the world's most divisively organized secondary school systems in one of the world's most unequal societies. Social class and race are mostly what's actually being measured. A young person from an intellectual/professional milieu who scores in the 85th percentile has not demonstrated anything at all, except perhaps laziness. A young person from a badly deprived background who scores in the 60th percentile is much more interesting and promising, and deserves not punishment (e.g., being "left back" or not admitted) but encouragement and commitment.

It's even more important to consider what else the tests don't measure. They do not measure almost all of a person's most important social capabilities: leadership ability, decisiveness, intuition, insight, originality, determination, and commitment to doing what one can do as well as one can do it. They do not measure, that is, *anything* that we'd be looking for if we were trying to create a genuine meritocracy as well as improve overall social product; quite the contrary.[18] They give no indication what society as a whole, that is general social utility, might expect from a person; and they give little indication how particular persons might benefit from an educational experience to which they were committed (except, as indicated, in the negative sense that educators would do well to be wary of people from privileged social backgrounds attaining only average test scores).

If tests were abolished or reined in, and the announced primary criterion for admission was how much the candidate seems likely to benefit from the education being offered, then these are the qualities admissions officers would look for in addition to grades, how well application essays were written, and so on. "Affirmative action" would not be an issue at those institutions attempting to make their student bodies more representative of the population at large, since there's no reason to believe that such qualities are more abundant in one subgroup than in another. It could only be an issue where there was an appearance of discrimination, but so-called reverse discrimination would simply disappear.

Given the continuation of existing social patterns, we can imagine that, for example, the "flagship" institutions of the California system, Berkeley and UCLA and their respective law and medical schools, would consequently enroll fewer Asian American students than are now qualifying for admission on the basis of SAT scores (and grades), and more African Americans or Hispanic Americans. Here we would indeed encounter a genuine problem of discrimination, precisely because these two universities announce themselves as "elite" to begin with, compared to the rest of the California system, and must somehow be able to justify that claim when challenged. *This* is the context in which "affirmative action" and "reverse discrimination" really do intersect, but the intersection occurs only because of the prior commitment of the state to straightforward elitism. (The same thing is true of the University of Texas Law School at Austin, where affirmative action has also been abolished.)

There are various grounds on which that commitment can be justified, but contribution to the realization of equal opportunity is not one of them. Elite institutions everywhere provide opportunity to those and only to those whose life histories fit best with development of the particular talent (or talents) that the going definition of "elite" apotheosizes. In part it is those life histories themselves that are the problem. First we (that is, people wielding market power in the United States) institute a steeply graded hierarchy of rewards for services rendered. We implement that hierarchy so that it discriminates, as it always has, on the basis of class, "race," and gender. This discrimination is then passed down, so to speak, to the next generation(s), who have less chance to develop the most highly rewarded talents because their parents are excluded from the life paths that emphasize those talents (although if a woman is married, and stays married to a man who has a relatively privileged place in that hierarchy, discrimination against her will not be passed down to her children). We then place all children in an educational system that usually (unlike Vaux Middle School) allocates few of its scarce resources to compensating for early childhood disadvantage—and discover, to our great surprise, that at an early age the patterns of accomplishment are generally replicating themselves, as evidenced by performance on "objective tests"; and that by college age that outcome seems to be irremediable.

But the complacent definition of "elite" or "best" is as much a part of the problem as is the structure of initial inequalities. Change that definition to emphasize instead, say, struggle against the odds, and much of the apparent conflict in implementation of our egalitarian principles disappears, even were the inegalitarian structure to remain in place. What does "equal opportunity" actually mean to us? Does it mean "equal opportunity for those with equally developed talents, and unequal opportunity for those with unequally developed talents"? Or does it mean "equal opportunity for those who put forth an equal effort, and unequal opportunity for those who put forth an unequal effort"?

Either answer to that question is justifiable. But the justifications are different. The former principle is strictly utilitarian, and in that sense is not really a principle. Its premise is that society will be more productive in some meaningful way if talent is rewarded and lesser talent is less rewarded. The latter principle is meritocratic; that is, it is based on the notion that reward has to be *earned*. To mix a modern metaphor with an ancient one, being born with a silver spoon is not the same as having a soul of silver. And the latter is, as far as we know, distributed generally and randomly, rather than on the basis of one's parents' social position.

Either answer can be justified, then. As I've already pointed out, the egalitarian ought not hesitate to stand with meritocracy as a principle of selection, for its instantiation would make most human societies much more equal than they are at present. Moreover, the problem with utilitarian analyses is that in the short run, the most useful—because the least costly—thing to do is always whatever has already been done; and the longer it's been done, the more useful to go on doing it in the same way, for the costs of changeover become tremendous. We never know what's going to happen in the long run anyway, so predictions about the long-term results of this or that policy are merely soothsaying.

That much being said, however, we must be clear whether we are talking about "fairness" or social utility when we attack *or* support compensatory social policy. Here again, the distinction between "rights" and "privileges" is paramount. If everyone has a "right" to attend the higher educational institution of his or her choice, it is certainly a most peculiar "right," for it is a right that has never been recognized or enforced in any polity. To institute such a "right" would be to overturn both merit *and* utility as decision-making principles; to treat going to college as though it were voting, or making a speech, or going to church.

Quite the contrary, in our ordinary understandings of the word, no one has a "right" to attend a particular educational institution, or any institution of higher learning in general. That is a privilege, contingent on the possession of certain kinds of credentials. What kinds of credentials legitimately bestow the privilege? In a democracy—that is, a system defined by the formal legal equality of all inhabitants—the obvious answer is, any credentials that are socially useful in general and useful to an admitting institution in particular, while not being morally suspect. Discriminatory credentials—that is, "credentials" consisting of having the right social background—are suspect; they are beyond the pale. The desire to have a diverse student body then is defensible without any difficulty on utilitarian grounds, only so long as it does not itself entail discrimination; that is, so long as students with specific social backgrounds fail to qualify because they do not add to "diversity," and are then replaced by others students who do.

The common complaint about affirmative action in higher education, of course, is that it *does* entail "reverse discrimination" in exactly that way: for example, denying some students entry to a particular institution *because* they are white.[19] So Rousseau's standard of "natural rectitude" is presumably betrayed. Identifiable persons, because they are specifically the *kinds* of persons they are, are being denied a publicly distributed privilege that is offered to others. How can this outcome be defended?

To confront this question, let us imagine a truly "color-blind" admissions process, in which no one knew *anything* about the social backgrounds of applicants.[20] How would the winning applicants be selected?

The most immediate answer is, Certainly not on the basis of SAT scores. Why on earth would any serious educational institution want its places to be monopolized by people who are good primarily at taking "objective" tests? Most boards of admissions really do seek "diversity" in a general way, after all. (Note, for instance, the stubborn and sometimes even apparently angry opposition of administrators at Berkeley and the University of Texas to the external mandate for the aboliton of affirmative action). To have only local students is to be seen as parochial, so at least at the undergraduate level both elite and nonelite institutions searching for diversity (as most nowadays are) would try to find students from different regions of the nation, from cities and rural areas as well as suburbs.

Outside a few select areas of the nation it is against the American grain to be visibly "elitist," so most institutions again would look for applicants from public as well as private schools within those cities and suburbs; students coming from working-class as well as professional families; and students needing scholarship assistance (because of which the admissions process can never be "class-blind"). Because colleges and universities derive prestige and even revenue from many other types of accomplishment beside the purely academic, they would also look for students who are good at the performing arts or athletics; or students who have shown leadership capacity of one kind or another; students with family members who attended the institution; and students who have overcome apparently limiting circumstances and demonstrated a special intensity of effort.

State colleges, community colleges, and universities would try to discover this diversity of experiences and talents within their state or local area. Even mediocre private schools drawing on primarily a local clientele would seek their own version of the same goal. Moreover, assuming no "open admissions" policy, virtually every type of institution could be expected to establish the same kind of limits: not to admit too many people who seem clearly unable to benefit from the kind of teaching that the faculty is used to offering (this limitation may suggest as much a criticism of faculties as of applicants) and to admit as many as possible applicants with the best purely academic credentials from the particular applicant pool, in order to maintain the academic reputation of the institution at its particular level. Putting all these different desiderata together, it is quite arguable that, deprived of the rationing shortcut of "objective" tests, American colleges and universities on the whole might well admit more nonwhite and working-class students than is now the case—and without any affirmative action at all.

What do we have now? Given a reliance solely on academic credentials that are distributed primarily by social background, the democratic intentions of higher education are devastated. As a whole the system takes on the look of a lexically scaled hierarchy. The "best" institutions have only the "best" (and thus disproportionately socially advantaged) students; the second best have only the second best students (disproportionately from somewhat less advantaged social backgrounds); and so on down the line. Diversity is not just a social good in its own right therefore; as I have noted above, its absence is also invariably an indication that discrimination, if in a more subtle form than in the past, remains firmly in place.

In sum, compensatory policy is necessary and justifiable in a nation such as the United States, It has also often been resoundingly successful in furthering equal opportunity of any kind, whether informally as in President Carter's appointments to the federal judiciary, or formally, as in the University of California's admissions policy.[21] However, the weight of inherited circumstances makes it difficult to implement that policy justly. Thus affirmative action as a particular version of compensatory social policy only takes on the appearance of wrongness because of a peculiar sequence of events. First, a public educational institution is dedicated to specifically elitist goals: as in the case of the University of California at Berkeley, for example, "creaming off" (along with UCLA) the top 10 percent of the state's high school graduates. Second, it announces that academic credentials in the form of test scores and high school grades (or rank) will be the primary determinants of who qualifies as "top tenth." Having taken these steps, it then denies admission to some marginal applicants who do nonetheless possess "top tenth" credentials, and for no other reason than that they are white (or Asian-Americans) are passed over in favor of applicants who do not. Normally expectable procedures *have* been overturned, and in such a way that injustice is seen to have occurred.

How could the legitimate goal of compensatory treatment be achieved without the policy's losing its "natural rectitude"? The first thing to note here is that the most acclaimed fallback position, affirmative action by class rather than race, has all the alleged vices of the latter, and no signal virtues of its own. To begin with, it does not in fact address the condition that affirmative action is intended to address. Being well-off may be a privilege, but no one thinks that the well-off are in any sense "better" (in the United States, reverse snobbery is much more common than the old-fashioned kind), and there is no generalized social resistance to the institutions—public schooling, scholarship aid—that make it easier for the less well-off to achieve their educational ends. Nor would any wealthy person dare be heard advocating that the poor not be admitted to college or graduate school.

Contrarily, with race (and with gender too in certain graduate programs, though fewer and fewer) there is a widespread presumption that being (especially) black or Hispanic is precisely to be inferior in an important sense, regardless of one's class position. Here, then, the distribution of credentials is thought by many people to distribute talents as well; the pseudoscientific industry to which I've already referred, its every meretricious "finding" faithfully reported by the *New York Times*'s "Science" section and *Book Review*, is devoted to that way of thinking. There is, then, a greater resistance to be overcome.

Moreover, the notion that reverse class favoritism is somehow more "fair" than any other kind has nothing to recommend it. Some of its proponents indeed suggest that it is a worse social fate to have poor white parents than to have middle-income black or Hispanic parents, and therefore more deserving of compensation; but this kind of comparison is as empty as it is odious. In any event, there is certainly no more "rectitude" in being rejected because of one's parents' income than because of one's skin color; the idea either that well-off applicants would feel better because the admissions process that had denied them was "color-blind," or that it's all right to treat people discriminatorily as long as they have money, is a transparent rationalization.

Confronting the real issue, we can see that there are simple short-term remedies to the paradox of color blindness, and complex long-term ones; and what they have in common is the recognition that so far we have been trying to achieve equal treatment on the cheap, and that cannot be done. Even in the nation that was first to dedicate immense resources to public education for all, we do not treat that sector with the gravity afforded national defense; we do not behave as though preparing all children to contribute the most they possibly can to overall social well-being is actually our goal. That is to say, affirmative action is only necessary because the American political system rewards other values—such as those derived from global domination—so much more than it does the search for equality of opportunity.

That is why my exploration of paths to diversity two pages above has to be phrased in the conditional tense: "might well admit." Primarily, the laissez-faire proposition that if we do nothing—if we don't discriminate and don't do anything to make sure we're not discriminating—then rectitude will automatically establish itself is really about levels of taxation, not principles of fairness. Here the reaction of affirmative action's opponents in California is indicative. Admitting that they're "troubled" by the quite shocking falloff in admissions to Berkeley after the passage of Proposition 209, several of them have insisted that they are still in the right, but that obviously "something has to be done" about the state of early and secondary education that has left so many black students so apparently ill prepared. Not a single one, though, has even mildly suggested rethinking California's limitations on the property tax, cutting back on the building of prisons, or taking any of the steps one might have to take to make such suggestions more than a manifest hypocrisy. Whatever the "trouble" is, it is not serious enough to force them to question their own fiscal priorities.

In contrast, if for a moment we were to stop asking what it would cost for a moment, and ask what ought to be done and what could fairly be done, then the most obvious short-term solution is institutional expansion. After all, students wish to attend elite schools for a very good and legitimate reason. Such schools are training grounds for membership in political, managerial, and professional elites; that is virtually their sole reason for existence, and in a society such as this one it is thus perfectly reasonable to seek upward social mobility by attending them.[22] That being so, the most obvious and legitimate strategy for schools such as Berkeley, UCLA, and the University of Texas at Austin is to define (as they were doing until forbidden) an appropriate number of "affirmative action" places, and then *add* those to previous (and expected) enrollment levels, rather than substituting them for places previously open to non—affirmative action candidates. To take a *reductio ad absurdum* case that illuminates the moral contours of this proposal: if at some time in the past discrimination had been instantly outlawed at a given school, and to implement the change one hundred nonwhite places were suddenly to be added to a previous enrollment of five hundred white persons, I would have nothing to complain about if I didn't make it as one of the five hundred.

Clearly, some such change is necessary in all democratic societies; but in the United States at least it would not be sufficient. The burden of the past here is a history not just of discriminatory exclusion but also of the gross, long-term, and enduring inequalities that have accompanied that history. *Those* inequalities—of living condition, of early childhood training and education, of available health care, of employment opportunities, of income security, of treatment by the law, of simply being counted the way everyone else is counted—are what effectively have to disappear before higher education can be the engine of change that we like to think of it as. The ultimate paradox is that strong equal opportunity not only must accompany but to some extent must precede the implementation of simple, fundamental fairness. It is in this respect—the continued existence of a racialized society and state—that the quintessentially American rhetoric of equal opportunity most outpaces its actual substance; and that we discover how entrenched the obstacles to equal opportunity can be.

7) WHY NOT EQUALITY?

The Retreat from Equality

To BE SELF-INTERESTED is perfectly reasonable; who else has one's interests at heart? The most important difficulty we confront in discussing equality, therefore, is not that so many people have seemingly come to oppose it in the name of their own interests, but rather that they appear to have sensible (not good, or truthful, but sensible) reasons for doing so. How has this come about?

The twentieth century saw the rise of mass, egalitarian politics; and is now witnessing a massive retreat from that same politics. The former phenomenon needs no further description. It is visible everywhere, even as its goal remains an absence: in the manifest difference between the way most people live out their lives in the advanced capitalist nations today and the way in which their parents and grandparents lived their lives in 1939 or 1914. Nor does it really need any explanation, for everywhere it was at first brought about by the same social forces: political parties (such as the New Deal Democratic Party in the United States) either organized by workers or representing them, and organized trade union movements. What has to be explained is the latter, and on the face of it curious, phenomenon: the retreat from equality.

To be sure, this has been not literally a "retreat." Everywhere capital has demanded that the postwar "social contract" of the Keynesian welfare state be broken; and the political class, whether initially reluctant or not, has ultimately acquiesced. And it is not that "the people" have welcomed the breaking of that implicit contract but that political leadership, most specifically the political leadership of the "Left," has given them no alternative; it has brought forth no leaders willing to mount a concerted resistance. The result has been that, for example, in the period since Ronald Reagan's first inauguration the United States has witnessed the greatest negative redistribution of wealth—from the poor to the rich—in recorded history; and this has come about almost without serious public discussion.

Casual discussions of this phenomenon usually begin with the term "globalization." But as I've suggested earlier, that word is only a description, and not a very satisfactory description, of contemporary, and truly counter-revolutionary, changes in the worldwide distribution of power and wealth since the mid-1970s. Unlike the earlier movement, it is not visibly producing a better way of life for people anywhere. In the affluent part of the world, its chief historical contribution so far is the destruction of the social-democratic or liberal Keynesian consensus of the postwar period.

Lack of popular resistance, or ineffectual popular resistance, to the forces promoting those changes is the apparent explanation of this phenomenon. But *why*, a few exemplary instances (in France most notably) aside, has there been so little mass counter-mobilization? Why does the party of equality, however defined, seem everywhere to be in retreat?

One answer to that question, although it is usually over-emphasized, cannot be evaded. In the United States more than anywhere else, but everywhere in some degree, there has been a general, across-the- board social demobilization, for the reason that contemporary mass media, most especially television, relentlessly privatize our *experience* of life at the same time that they nationalize and even internationalize our *images* of it. Most quantitative research on what television does to our thinking has no credibility, in that it assumes without warrant an extreme malleability of people's intellects and an almost demonic long-term irresistibility of mediocre visual productions. However, the most credible research also fairly consistently produces a finding based on no such assumptions about people's alleged propensity to be "brainwashed," but rather suggests that the more time people devote to watching television, the less likely they are to develop a strong, consistent interest in public political life (or the more likely never to develop such an interest). Television, that is, does not so much change our consciousness as colonize it; to distract viewers from any kind of contemplation except what pertains to immediate material consumption (especially of itself) is commercial television's sole, and apparently all-too-obtainable, goal.[1]

This is undoubtedly an important component of late-twentieth-century life, especially in the United States, but it is not a satisfying explanation of large-scale political events. Ideology can only play its role if it is in tune with what is going on in the world. Thus we need to know what *is* going on that makes political demobilization seem to so many people to be a rational response to the world around them.

The answer to that question has two parts. The first of them may seem a little evasive, in that in consists of an assertion that the extent of the retreat from egalitarianism has been greatly overstated. If we just look at the United States, for example, where the rout is supposed to be most complete, what we find in the past forty years is an astonishing extension of popular doctrines of equality, as well as a tremendous assertion of local and communal demands in the public arena. In the United States again, the intense popular mobilizations of first the civil rights movement and then the feminist revolution, decisively broadened understandings of what it means to "participate" in politics. The New Left of the 1960s has in fact won its philosophical battle decisively. The ideas that you can't fight City Hall, that complex decisions are best left to the experts, and that distant representatives can be counted on to get us what we want and need have been seriously weakened, if not demolished beyond recovery. The nuclear power industry elite, among many others, could testify to this effect in the United States; but even in as centralized and elitist a polity as Great Britain it has been necessary to resurrect virtually tyrannical doctrines of authoritarian force in order to accomplish the once-simple public task of road building, in the face of mass, direct resistance to the bulldozers.

Substantively as well, in the United States both constitutional doctrine and public policy have been extended well beyond earlier New Deal understandings of what it means to provide "equal rights" and "equal opportunity." As I've pointed out in discussing affirmative action, there is no obvious dividing line between "equal opportunity" traditionally defined as formally equal rights and strong equal opportunity, or rights supported by a realistic chance of realizing their promise. In the United States, as opposed to say, Sweden, this larger understanding of equality is very far from encompassing the full conception of strong equal opportunity. Still, to the extent that American liberal ideology has begun to cross that line, then it has not at all been dispelled by racial or sexual "backlash." Instead, it has actually been internalized throughout the American polity—so much so, that the greatest obstacle to opportunity for minorities has come to be the insistence by majorities that they too have an "equal right" to that same, newly defined, "opportunity."

White applicants to colleges assert that affirmative action denies them equality of treatment, but before the civil rights revolution hardly anyone would have thought to claim that access to higher education was a "right" at all. Men assert the right not to have female supervisors deny them career opportunities by insisting that they provide sexual favors ("sexual harassment")—the common experience of women in every walk of life before the apotheosis (not just in the United States) of late-twentieth-century feminism. As events at the Citadel and Virginia Military Institute exemplify, advocates of returning women to the home give the general appearance of canoeists paddling against a tidal wave. The same is true, no matter how much they may seem to achieve temporary local successes, of those who want to keep "America" a white, English-speaking nation as a matter of principle. Even the doctrine of equal rights for gay people, an unfathomable concept not so long ago, dominates public discourse about homosexuality; and outside the hierarchy of the Catholic Church opponents of abortion rights are much more likely to refer to the "rights" of the fetus than they are to talk about the sacredness of life. Neither in the United States nor anywhere else (except perhaps the fundamentalist Islamic world) does there seem to be any turning back from these extensions, where they have taken hold, of the egalitarian movement.

At the same time, the halt in the onward march of *economic* egalitarianism is unmistakable, and this is the second part of the answer we are seeking. It was the democratization of economic policy sponsored by the mass organizations of labor that everywhere set the stage for whatever minorities and feminists have accomplished in the last third of this century. If those organizations and the energy they expressed are now in decline, that is surely because massed labor itself, their human base, is really in decline.

The past three decades have witnessed an immense and unmistakable decomposition of labor; the bellwether industries of monopoly capital that produced the welfare state as a response—coal, steel, auto manufacturing, transportation, construction—no longer occupy the high ground of capitalist progress. There's nothing particularly radicalizing about any of these versions of industrial labor taken by itself; what was radicalizing about them was that, taken together, they provided a common experience of making a living that seemed, at some times at least, to represent everyone's experience. This was never literally true, of course, and no labor party, except in Sweden, ever came close to holding a monopoly of political power. But it was true enough that even if the forces of labor did not constitute a majority, they did constitute a cohesive, and exemplary, plurality. Although not in the revolutionary sense intended by Marx, the working class appeared as "a class . . . which has radical chains," as "a sphere of society which has a universal characters because its suffering is universal."[2]

As that common experience of monopoly capital and high industrialism has disappeared, the idea of wage laborers as a representative class has become chimerical, and the notion that "their" party is the people's party impossible to sustain. Moreover, in the United States (not it alone by any means) the further fracturing of an already fractured work force along racial lines has only deepened the general Western tendency. The embracing of George Wallace by a significant proportion of the old New Deal coalition in 1968 defined a voting and social realignment that continues to dominate American politics and that has not yet played itself out.

And yet, sociological currents do not produce political outcomes by themselves; there have to be reasons why they result in one kind of political movement rather than another. Even the "race card" will only produce reactionary politics if there is some good reason for it to do so; that is, if some benefit is to be gained from reactionary politics. Here, it is an intersection of social forces with concomitant structural tendencies that demands our attention. Although these structural considerations do not apply with equal force everywhere, they especially help explain why the general retreat is so frantic in the United States.

The concrete politics of equality is arguably a function of three structural factors. The first of these is the absolute distance between social classes and groups. The second is the extent and depth of poverty; the third is the average income of social groups. Where, as in the United States, there is a high average income, great poverty, and a great (absolute and relative) distance between the poor and those who like to think of themselves as "middle class," then even the most basic redistributive policies will feel more costly to middling taxpayers; and thus in the short term will affect a majority of (mostly white) voters negatively (or so they might rationally think).[3] Taxation will come to seem not taking from the rich to give to the poor, but taking from the middle to "give" to the poor (who in the United States are, again, incorrectly perceived to be mostly nonwhite). From the origins of the "tax revolt" in California two decades ago to the present day, this tendency has been unstoppable, like a juggernaut rolling downhill.[4]

As I shall argue, the politics of equality, and the only politics compatible with an egalitarian movement, is the politics
of solidarity; and this is exactly what vanishes, at least relatively speaking, as the uneven development imposed by
capitalism opens up what are perceived by many as irrepa-
rable fissures in the common life. The experience and thus
the politics of uneven development in, say, Mexico, Brazil,
even Japan, and the United States, merely replicates the experience and thus the politics of uneven development in
New York City or in Orange County. As perceptions of social
distance replace any sense of affiliation, contempt becomes
the dominant political emotion, and intergroup conflict the
dominant way of life.

All of these conditions are worsened, furthermore, by the
general (in the West) slowdown in economic growth since
the first oil-price "break" of 1973. As various commentators
have pointed out, for example, the "mere" 1 percent falloff
in average growth rates from the decade of the 1970s
through the decade of the 1980s represents hundreds of billions of dollars in "lost" production, employment, and
household consumption values. A declining rate of growth,
even if the rate itself remains positive, is thus perceived almost instantly. It is as though eight people sitting around a
dinner table, each happily contemplating the large piece of
pie that is about to cap the meal, suddenly discover that
there are only seven servings to be divided up. They're
friends, presumably, and anyway it's only dessert. But if instead they are arms-length acquaintances and sometime
competitors for the allocation of general welfare, and the
"pie" represents an entire material way of life, then the process of reapportionment that now develops is not going to be
friendly. Nor has it been.

It may seem paradoxical to suggest that redistributive

movements are likely to fare better in an era of good feeling, if one accepts Lenin's dictum that "the worse the better." But the oppressiveness of general scarcity only produces bare-knuckled competition and the politics of envy. It is not possible to build an egalitarian social order on the foundation of envy, not even on envy of the wealthy. This is not simply because envy is corrosive, although that is certainly the case. There is a more profound difficulty. Envy is only another version of legitimized greed, upon which the values and incentives of a society that produces great but unequally distributed wealth were founded to begin with. All too quickly envy resolves into rancor toward those on the bottom as well as those on the top. The poor and excluded, who for whatever reasons are unable to engage in the kind of decently paid labor that is the presumed norm in capitalist societies, are typecast as "sponges," "idlers," "parasites." In their expulsion from the institutions of waged work they are as much a reproach to the envious as are the very rich. Everywhere in the advanced capitalist world today, this middle-class resentment often results not in the politics of equality but instead in right-wing, authoritarian populism.[5]

This rightward movement in turn leads in profoundly ugly directions: toward a politics of racial contempt, moral hostility, and sexual hysteria. This politics is much worse than the ordinary conservative politics of complacent utilitarianism: "I've got enough, and it couldn't get better for anybody without getting worse for everybody." It includes the perceptions that "race" is an insoluble problem, any solution to "the woman question" must be unacceptable to hard-working people, and sexual "license" is the work of the devil. The spread of such perceptions doesn't have to be overwhelming; it merely has to be widespread enough to upset previous voting patterns and call into question whatever position of dominance or influence the parties of egalitarianism have previously achieved.

It's possible to share any of those beliefs and not make a fuss about it. Few readers of these pages (and I include their author) would not be embarrassed if our unexpurgated, wayward thoughts about others could be taped and replayed to the general public. But to say that is not to endorse, not even in the slightest degree, any notion of inevitable group hostility and conflict in social life. Prejudice against "the other" may be endemic, but in some circumstances it will produce nothing more than occasional moments of personal discomfort. As the saying goes, some of my best friends are anti-Semites; and some of their best friends are Jews. Even where the denigration of a "race" is built into the entire fabric of life, as in the United States, its social effects can be damped down and gradually attenuated (think of professional sports) if other conditions do not make its institutionalization useful to large numbers of people and therefore historically necessary. When those "other conditions" loom as large as they do now, however, people—even otherwise well-intentioned people—will begin freely to deploy their casual stereotypes in public, and with dangerous results.

To take one precise example: in her *Alchemy of Race and Rights*, Patricia Williams describes an incident in which she rings the bell of one of those Soho boutiques to which admission is only granted on request; the owner comes to the door, peers out at her, sees an apparently African American woman, and promptly closes the shutter.[6] This is American racism still at work, quite clearly, despite the insistence of affirmative action opponents that it is really a thing of the past. However, it is also important to note that we actually learn little from the tale about the boutique's proprietor herself. It is quite possible, for example, that at some other time or place (say, Northampon, Massachusetts today) another person much fuller of traditional racial prejudice than this particular proprietor is, might have readily granted admission to Williams, while keeping her own disdainful thoughts to herself.

What potentially makes the difference is a particular historical conjunction. The overt, public politics of white supremacy, embraced by the Republican Party as the centerpiece of its attempt to achieve political hegemony, comes together with the carefully nurtured "moral panic" about street crime that marks New York City, where Williams's story takes place. The real, unavoidable result of a politics of racial oppression and exclusion—impoverished people tend to engage in street crime at a higher rate than do well-off white people—is turned into a generalized hysteria, by a political party and mass media both attempting to use an economic crisis to their own advantage. In such times, even *soi-disant* "liberal" New Yorkers—for all we know that proprietor might have been one of them—turn into embattled defenders of skin privilege.

Turning a stereotype into a threat, whites become meaner. We are much too familiar with the result today: a kind of psychic arms race in which all parties feel aggrieved. Whites (the behavior of New York City's popular Mayor Giuliani is instructive) behave as though any emotional disarmament would be unilateral; nonwhites, seeing no white persons apparently worthy of their trust, quite logically respond in kind. In such a poisonous atmosphere social policy itself, let alone genuinely egalitarian social policy, comes to seem unmakable; doing nothing ("benign neglect") appears to be the most rational course of action. In the absence of any sense of social solidarity, the move toward more equality stalls.

"That aspect of the modern crisis which is bemoaned as a 'wave of materialism' is related to what is called the 'crisis of authority,'" wrote one of this century's great Marxist theorists in the 1920s:

> If the ruling class has lost its consensus, i.e. is no longer "leading" but only "dominant," exercising coercive force alone, this means precisely that the great masses have become detached from their traditional ideologies, and no longer believe what they used to believe previously, etc. The crisis consists precisely in the fact that the old is dying and the new cannot be be born; in this interregnum a great variety of morbid symptoms appear.[7]

Change a few phrases, and Antonio Gramsci's diagnosis remains as concrete and relevant today as it was then. In the contemporary crisis, when the unresponsive political and economic institutions provide no rational outlet for our fears and desires, all the execrescences of our halfhearted pluralism, which might well by now have become but its vestigial remains, instead have become "morbid symptoms" of social decay.[8]

The problem is worst of all in the United States. That is not only because of the endemic racialization of politics; nor even because American political institutions are specifically and uniquely designed (as James Madison explained and justified in the tenth Federalist Paper) to forestall rather than enable the formation of decisive majorities. More crucially, the American business elite has made even less room than business elites usually do for expressions of working-class solidarity and has devoted its immense resources and global power to bending both major political parties to its will. Since representatives of the corporate elite approached President Carter in 1978 with the message that American capital could no longer afford the social contract (and that the Democratic Party would not be funded if it went on defending that contract), what I've so far called the retreat from equality has been a staged retreat. One might say that the corporate capitalist class, now in control of both parties, has retreated the people; the people have been retreated.

Institutions are indeed important. Only in wartime or during an all-enveloping crisis such as that of the Great Depression has the American system of federalized and separated powers and decentralized political parties fostered the aggregation of majority interests for more than merely defensive purposes. But still, the breaking of the social contract has not been unique to the United States nor to the United States and the other "Anglo-Saxon" democracies. In the end, the underlying historical problem of capitalism shows its effects in every corner of the globe. It sweeps everything before it and yet has nothing to show for itself but a massively unequal, and frighteningly insecure, distribution of merely material rewards.

Competing Solidarities

An egalitarian society, however, cannot be founded on merely materialistic premises. It can only be founded in deeply held feelings of social solidarity—social solidarity of the particular kind that results in collaborative political activity. What is this solidarity?

It begins in recognition that the so-called atomized individual of classical liberal ideology is a myth. That myth has been treated as a reality, of course, by the free market ideologues who find it useful in furthering their own economic interests. But it has also been ascribed an undeserved status of reality by its opponents. Whether they be traditional Marxists wanting to criticize capitalism or latter-day communitarians wanting to criticize liberal pluralism, these opponents have found it useful to ascribe to their enemy (capitalism, liberalism) something that is manifestly not true: that it *creates* "atomized individuals." On the contrary: capitalism (for the Marxist critics of capitalism are much more correct than the communitarian critics of liberalism) *pulverizes* both communities and thus individuals. It never, however, succeeds in eliminating their fundamental connection; which is not local and parochial, as the communitarians have it, but human.

There is indeed solidarity; there is indeed a General Will. It would be a strange individual who has never had the experience of voluntarily submitting his or her own desires to those of a more general sociality. More precisely, however, there are competing solidarities—of nation, community, religion, ethnicity, gender, sexuality, class—and many general wills, not just one. Rather than surrendering themselves to some preestablished unity, the goal of egalitarians is to forge a unity out of many solidarities.

To suggest that this might be easy would be the thinnest pretense. We have already seen how historically burdened perceptions of racial difference can divide an entire polity and how class distance can fracture a mass political movement. The example of two other, equally burdensome types of divisive solidarity makes this point even more clear, for many of us accept them without even the faintest intellectual unease.

The first of these has to do with the geographical boundaries of equality among peoples. I do not mean by this the familiar and conventional question of what *nations*, or the peoples who compose them, owe each other; that is just a matter of *realpolitik*, once the assumption of multiple and competing nationhood has been accepted without reservation. I mean to ask instead the quite different question: what do *individuals* who live in separate national jurisdictions owe each other?[9] If a majority of the U.S. Congress, genuinely representing a majority of the American people, had voted to declare war on North Vietnam, would that have made it "right"? Who should have participated in that vote? As Robert Nozick has remarked, there's no intellectually principled reason for stopping majority rule at the water's edge. Again, I know that the shirt I buy labeled Made in Indonesia is made by viciously oppressed, mostly female labor, but do I have any obligations of solidarity with those women, such as I felt with "American" farm laborers during the various produce boycotts called by Cesar Chavez's farm workers union?

Clearly, any consideration of such questions by me or any other inhabitant of the world's most technologically advanced and powerful capitalist society can only be partial and painfully tentative. It can only take off from, and build on, the work of those spokespersons who can genuinely try to speak for what Fanon called "les damnees de la terre," because they have inhabited the same lifeworld as, or at the very least lived side by side with, those people whose material needs are so often markedly different from, and vastly greater than, the expressed needs of the Western working class.[10]

From this very limited "First World" standpoint, the beginning of any answer to the questions I've asked above is obviously that, the artificiality of national boundaries aside, my most immediate obligations are to those persons who have an historical reason to expect them from me, and who might be expected to feel similar obligations to me in return. But that's only the beginning of an answer. The boundaries are still artificial, historical tradition or not, compared to the unavoidable universality of any ethical principle, such as the principle of equality. It's no use saying, as Michael Walzer and other communitarians say, that principles of justice must be based on "shared understandings" and that therefore justice is primarily local; or that, as various postmodernists assert, ideals such as "justice" and "equality" are nothing but socially variable linguistic constructions.[11] Stated so baldly, neither of these positions is tenable.

Quite to the contrary, I would suggest that there's not an iota of misunderstanding, linguistic or historical, between Indonesian workers who think that they are oppressed by domestic tyranny and exploited by Western imperialism and American economists and industrialists who preach the rationality of market choice and "comparative advantage." If representatives of each group were to read Marx (as some of them probably have), whether in a common language or in separate translations, they would all understand him perfectly well. They would have intellectual disagreements (is the labor theory of value defensible, and can a notion of fair exchange be founded on it?), and practical disagreements based on considerations of self-interest and power. But neither group would have the faintest doubt that they were arguing about the nature of economic justice, and neither would be influenced in any great degree by purely local traditions or by varying semiotic codes.

You own it, I don't own it, and you say that therefore you can do anything you want with it, even if I am badly injured by your actions. This language is a universal language par excellence, and it's understood and resisted as such in every corner of the globe. Summing up examples of resistance and revolutionary practice (on a small scale) from all over the globe, two critics of "globalization" conclude:

If capitalist globalization is an infection, it can be said to coexist with many other types of infection. Were we not bedazzled by images of the superior morphology of global capitalism, it might be possible to theorize the global integration of noncapitalist economic relations and noneconomic relations to see capitalist globalization as coexisting with, and even facilitating, the renewed viability of noncapitalist globalization.[12]

The exact nature of the resistance will certainly be based on particularistic traditions—Walzer's "shared understandings." The communal decentralism of the Indian village, for example, produces a different idea of what ought to be done than do the Jacobinism and Bonapartism of France; but this is a difference about how, not whether, to pursue a commonly understood goal.[13]

In the same way, many Afghani or Irani women reading Mary Wollstonecraft's *Vindication of the Rights of Women* or Mill's *The Subjection of Women* for the first time might well reject their argument. But many others would accept it (and have accepted it); and in any case every female reader would know exactly what Mill, for instance, meant when he wrote, "I consider it presumption in any one to pretend to decide what women are or are not, can or cannot be, by natural constitution. They have always been hitherto kept, as far as regards spontaneous development, in so unnatural a state, that their nature cannot but have been greatly distorted and disguised . . ."[14] The principles of ideologically inspired dismissal on the one hand, and of logical reasoning on the other, are again universally visible; and the notion of equality that they reject or to which they appeal varies only in the details of its implementation, never in its core meaning.

To put these two examples as one, the Indonesian or Philipine women who are conscripted as women (by husbands, by fathers, and often by armed force) into literal wage sla-

very, brutalized by local tyrants, exploited by overseas corporations, and ignored by happy American consumers are
being subjected to a much harsher version of the same regi-
men, based on the same sexual division of labor, as are
American women conscripted into "paid work" by "welfare
reform." If notions of equality are thought by American social critics to demand that those Americans who benefit
from the exploitation of female labor abolish the conditions
in which it is exploited, how can that demand not weigh
even more heavily on those of us who benefit (as we all in
fact do) from its much more horrific version? And if, more
generally, we seek to limit the power of American-based corporations to close factories or to poison workers in Ohio or
Illinois or North Carolina, then how can we not seek the
same control over what those corporations do in Indonesia or
the Philipines or Brazil?

Of course we, whoever we are, can't fix the whole world
and ought not even to try. In the post-Reagan era, after all,
most Americans have yet to put up any significant resistance
to the despoiling of lives, neighborhoods, and the natural
environment by corporations operating right in front of our
eyes. Here Walzer is certainly correct: wherever the search
for justice may lead us ultimately it does begin, like charity,
at home. The notion that "we" should investigate working
conditions in Indonesia and then shouldn't buy shirts made
there but that it's all right to buy chickens raised and killed
by exploited workers in North Carolina or Maine without
paying any great attention to what goes on in their employment is incoherent. And few people will be impressed by it.

I do not intend these remarks as an argument about what
policies the United States should adopt; overseas workers
probably look to the American Congress with about the
same degree of hope that sheep would feel in the presence of

a convocation of wolves. The argument, rather, is about what principles egalitarians have to advocate and stand by. For there is a coherent principle at stake here: the case against the exploitation of one is ineluctably a case against the exploitation of all. Obversely, the case for more equality is a case for the greater equality of all, not just of a favored few. Whatever legislative or cultural changes egalitarians in the rich nations of the globe advocate, therefore, at a minimum have to advance the interests of the most exploited and the least advantaged *wherever* they might be found.

There is certainly a limitation on what might be intended by that last assertion. Whatever those "alien" interests are, we must understand them at first in an abstract and institutional form. Most of us who aren't saints can't live our lives in single-minded dedication to the world's poorest people, nor can or should any American policy-makers, even if some day they might truly be egalitarians themselves, try to fine-tune either legislation or trade policies so as to serve the interests of oppressed workers in Jakarta. Instead, the universality of the principle of equality has two implications at a minimum.

First, neither the well-off nor even the poor deserve support if they try to better their material condition at the expense of those who are worse off than they are. Second, those who struggle (or say they struggle) to create, maintain, or improve institutions of democratic equality in their own polity ought to show their solidarity with those who struggle for those goals anywhere else; or else we are visibly confusing a class interest with a general one. More concretely, this means that American (or German or Swedish) egalitarians considering the condition of the working classes in Indonesia or the Philipines or Brazil and their obligations to those classes would have to remind themselves of the following realities when rendering any analysis of American (or German etc.) political economy.

Workers in the United States and other Western capitalist societies possess the basic civil liberty of the right to vote and in some more limited degree the rights to organize unions and to bargain collectively; as well as (in the United States) various compensatory protections such as those created by the National Labor Relations Act of 1936, the Fair Labor Standards Act of 1940, the Occupational Safety and Health Act, the Civil Rights Act of 1964, and so on. All of these rights and protections (except the vote) have been under severe threat in the United States since their inception, and most have been seriously curtailed. They still exist in principle, however, and organized labor struggles to defend and extend them. The obligation of American labor (or any organized Western European labor) and its supporters is therefore to encourage and (if called upon to do so) aid, all struggles of overseas labor for those same institutions.

By the same token, most women in the West effectively have the right not to be sold into wage slavery, not to be conscripted into prostitution, and not to be excluded from legal protections available to male workers. Again, for many women these rights are under threat, or at least lack effective enforcement; but their condition is the exception rather than the rule. In contrast, working-class or rural women in many poor countries (where, as Cynthia Enloe has remarked, "cheap labor" is really a euphemism for subjugated female labor), are subject to all those oppressions, without any recourse to the law.[15] American and other Western egalitarians, and certainly those who work for sexual equality, are consequently obliged to support the struggles of women in poorer countries to achieve simple, formal, legal equality.

There is a serious problem here, however, in all the Western capitalist societies but especially in the United States. Although the American state is complicit with capital against the interests of American workers, it does function to protect those workers whenever their economic interests are coterminous with those of capital. In fact, despite the passage of NAFTA the American state is still one of the most protectionist states in the world, and organized American workers on the whole fight for more rather than less protection against overseas or multinational capital. This can be seen not only in requests for tariff protection generally, but in, for example, the effort to require Mexico to incorporate labor legislation as part of NAFTA.

One would think that the American labor movement ought to consider itself duty bound, therefore, to support rather than to oppose the protectionism of labor movements in poorer countries with poorer working classes: sauce for the gander. But this is not as simple a demand as it sounds. American economic nationalists (not all but some of whom will be found in the labor movement) often formulate the problem of poor economies in the concept of competition from "cheap labor," an evidently racist and sexist formulation that has the rhetorical effect of blaming the exploited rather than those who exploit them. Genuine solidarity with those who supply "cheap labor" is unthinkable; it would be like solidarity with scabs. Conversely, from the standpoint of exploited labor and peasant agriculture in the non-Western world, the chief exploiter, hiding behind the veil of the "multinational corporation," is American capital itself, which still dominates world financial and consumer markets and with which American labor has reached at least a partial accommodation.

In the poorer countries of the world, the "success" of global capitalism is for local elites and a minority of workers only. To most others the global market brings devastation and dislocation in its wake, and in the absence of a nationalist revolution governments can usually be counted on to be nothing more than a brutal occupying army for overseas capital. Though there may be a commonality of interest between American workers who don't want their jobs exported overseas and overseas workers and villagers who don't want to be raped by the penetrations of American capital, the latter are often in the position of resisting and attacking precisely that which is "American." Their consequent interpretation of the global capitalist world as an evil American empire is as alien and unacceptable to most American ears as it is accurate.

From an egalitarian standpoint, however, "anti-Americanism" (and sometimes, though not as often, anti-Westernism in general) is the very essence of the overseas working-class and peasant struggle against domination by capital. The struggle for more equality, therefore, requires an understanding of the world's super-exploited masses, including also the often nonwhite and bitterly resented reserve army of labor in the United States, not as "cheap labor" but as "oppressed labor." More, it requires the spirit of solidarity with those oppressed in their struggles rather than of resentment against them as labor market competitors, even if that is to an extent what they inevitably must be.

Undoubtedly, for specific people this may not always be possible. There is a serious issue, for example, posed by the problem of immigration. When well-off Californians support legislation depriving "illegal aliens" of their ordinary human rights ("illegal" according to whose laws and according to what concept of national boundaries?), thereby securing for themselves a labor pool of defenseless, indentured domestic servants, their position is so transparently hypocritical as to be morally indefensible. But African American workers (or would-be workers) in Southern California who support the same legislation are genuinely trying to protect themselves against a competition that on the whole they cannot withstand.

Still, it's essential for all of us, including even those who seem to be bearing the major costs of immigration, to be aware that among the reasons Mexican (and other Central American and Caribbean) workers come to the United States in such large numbers are that in their national homelands they lack certain basic legal protections and economic rights taken for granted even in the capitalist United States, and that the industrial, agricultural, and natural resource sectors that super-exploit their labor do so under the protective umbrella of an American economic policy and imperial politics that has always subjected Central America to a subordinate status. And it's also crucial for all of us to be aware that it's the historical racism of the American polity, economy, and labor movement that has forced many African Americans into the position of hapless competitor for the lowest rung on the economic ladder; not the nasty competitive nature of Latin Americans with whom they must ultimately be allies.

The never-ending, unstoppable flow of Mexican citizens (and of course U.S. citizens too, although for different reasons) across what is in reality a purely notional, totally porous border, suggests an underlying unity of persons and lives beneath apparent fragmentation. Since, as I've noted, both African American citizens of the United States and Latin American citizens of its neighbors to the south have experienced the historical disaster of being relegated to the margins by uneven economic and political development, they have both suffered the same frustration and deprivation—that is, the denial of fundamental human needs.[16]

To ignore this underlying equivalence is again to try to gain equality on the cheap, rather than confront its real history, its real enemies, and its real costs. To substitute a politics based on group envy for a politics based on recognizable human need is to ensure failure. Turned against each other, the oppressed become blackmailers of each other on behalf of those who benefit from their joint enmity. Contrarily, the principle of solidarity based on recognition of human need knows no boundaries.

Solidarity, I have insisted, is the fundamental ethos of equality. Surely, though (Marx to the contrary), we cannot expect an international solidarity of workers of the same intensity as those local solidarities entrenched by centuries of national development. That is true. But if the spirit of egalitarian solidarity is not extended, at least in principle, to those who are exploited by institutions that most of us in the affluent world, even wage workers, think of as "our own," the movement for more equality will self-destruct. It cannot survive in the face of mortal competition among those who seek it.

The second example of partial solidarities is sexual solidarity, seemingly less global in its scope and effects than the division of nations, but in fact also a crucial obstacle to the pursuit of equality. Again, it often goes unrecognized that sexual solidarity is a two-way affair. It becomes noticed when women oppose their mistreatment by men (e.g., "feminism") or the gender hierarchy of state and society. But as Shannon Faulkner could testify, an exclusive and often oppressive kind of masculine solidarity stands behind that mistreatment.

Male solidarity comes in many guises. Most familiarly, a certain kind of sexual solidarity exists among men in occupations based mostly on physical strength or at least physical performance.[17] Among these men this sexual solidarity often passes for class solidarity, but the truth about this solidarity is revealed by its targets of choice. Assertive women, gays, and "pansy intellectuals" are as much as or more its enemy than capitalists, since the behavior of the former has more resonance in those aspects of life within the average man's immediate control. Who will do the dishes, what makes a good movie, what's worth doing on a Friday night, and above all what makes a man a "real man"—these issues, the immediately observable material of daily life, can easily define one's entire world. Even among men in the learned professions (see my comment about surgeons in chapter 6), legitimate authority is more often than not associated with the ability to demonstrate (or intimate) physical force, and masculinity with the power not to have one's decisions be subjected to a woman's judgment. In every social class, of course, these temptations of manhood have diminished in the wake of the feminist revolution; but they remain as bastions of privilege and major obstacles to a wider solidarity.

Women's sexual solidarity is not as focused as men's, since women's labor is rarely as collectivized. It tends to be strongest in the nonwage realms of life, and is on the whole a defensive reflex rather than an aggressive opposition. But most of all, female sexual solidarity, unlike its male counterpart, does prefigure a more encompassing, and more egalitarian, solidarity. The solidarity of those who demand the end of privilege, unlike the solidarity of those who struggle to maintain it, can (and sometimes does) lead beyond itself. On some occasions at least feminist solidarity has consisted of the effort to forge a common bond out of competing solidarities among women. Just so, egalitarian politics consists of the effort, as manifested both in the kinds of policies described in chapter 4 and in interventions aimed at counter-ideological persuasion, to forge a common bond out of these competing, more parochial, solidarities.

How this is to be done in practice, however, is obviously the concern of activists more than theorists. To become more than simply an abstract theory, the theory of equality awaits a mass movement founded on the politics of equality (that is, democratic participation) to demand it; and leaders committed to democratic participation, to help that mass movement define itself. We can only guess what will be the issues that unite various peoples who are now united in that movement. They will almost certainly be issues around which people in different nations and from widely differing backgrounds will be able to congregate, having to do with the penetration of daily life, space, and culture by the aggressive, impersonal, and unforgiving institutions of global capital.

8) CONCLUSION:
EGALITARIAN SOLIDARITY

W HAT THEORY CAN TELL US, if not *how* to forge common bonds, is *what* kind of sentiment would have to undergird them. I say "sentiment" because it is essential to understand that a transformative egalitarian politics can never be based merely on strategic considerations: "you and I must form a coalition, because neither of us can separately gain our desired ends." If the parties to a coaliton are simply using each other, it will break up in fairly short order. Only some kind of mutual recognition, of equality and in equality, can make an egalitarian coaliton work. What kind of mutual recognition must that be?

To begin with, it is crucial to distinguish the egalitarian sentiment from some others that look like it, and are often mistaken for it, but are actually far from being the same thing. Egalitarian politics is motivated, always, by outrage at the disparity between the lives of those who possess an immense superfluity and of those many millions more who lack even a bare sufficiency. It is a moral outrage generated, as I have remarked, by the fact that the disparity can be justified neither by any apparent social necessity nor by any apparent difference in deservingness among the groups who benefit and suffer from it. But this mobilizing sense of outrage, when it is truly general, is based not so much on my envy of he who has more than I do, as on my sorrow for she who has less. Solidarity is not mass envy. It is the sentiment behind Franklin Roosevelt's declaration quoted earlier, that "a civilization is judged not by how much it gives to those who already have a lot, but by how much it gives to those who have little"; behind Eugene Debs's famous assertion that "while there is a lower class, I am in it; while there is a criminal element, I am of it; while there is a soul in prison, I am not free"; and behind the political theorist Christian Bay's simple statement that "a society is as free as its under-dogs are."[1] The Swedish welfare state, again, worked so well for so long because it was concretely rooted in this kind of sentiment: the L. O., the national labor organization, struck a comprehensive collective bargaining agreement with Swedish industry, the essence of which was that the first goal of all wage settlements—the "wage solidarity policy" as it has been called—was to narrow the gap between the best paid and the worst paid.[2]

Thus we see that this kind of solidarity is also not merely collective economic interest. Class interests certainly do exist everywhere, and they cause trouble for social cohesion (from the standpoint of those who benefit unreservedly from it). But the solidarity that grows out of expressed or activated interests, such as those mobilized by a strike, is usually localized; and if more than that, rarely lasts very long beyond the occasion. Only where massed workers have implemented some version of the general strike, as in Sweden in 1931 or the United States in 1936–37, has the result of labor action been system-challenging legislation.[3] Still, the enveloping sense of a general interest soon dissolves into the fragmentary interests that momentarily came together.

In contrast, egalitarian solidarity, which exists much more rarely, does not depend on short-term and occasional mobilizations. As we learn from the Swedish example, this kind of solidarity requires what we might a call a certain disposition.[4] It is the disposition to ally oneself with others not because they are similar to oneself in social background or agree with one's own tastes and values but precisely because they are different *and yet* have permanently common human interests. It is the mutual recognition of *these* interests, not the mere recognition of being in the same economic or social position, that defines solidarity among equals.

Without this sense of mutual recognition, as well as the sentiment of empathy that underlies it, a mass politics of resentment is possible but egalitarian politics is not. These are not, of course, attitudes addressed toward humanity at large, in some vague generalities that lead to a politically demobilizing inability to distinguish between allies and enemies. Equality, even when defined narrowly, has numerous and important enemies; these cannot be wished out of existence and they are owed no more respect or civility than the forcefulness of their own enmity and opposition suggests.

The solidarity required of egalitarian politics is instead *solidarity with all one's potential allies*. These allies, it ought to go without saying, have to be numerous enough to form a substantial majority when an egalitarian movement has reached its full potential. Otherwise it can't be an egalitarian movement, for the basic decision-making procedure of equality is majority rule, in that no other decision-making procedure treats all those putatively subject to its decisions as formally equal. As I have noted earlier, whereas minority *right* is fundamental to equality, minority *rule* in the name of equality is a contradiction in terms, since at the very least it rules out the achievement of *political* equality.[5]

What then ought we to mean by these constituent terms, mutual recognition and empathy? We can approach an answer to that question by thinking about so-called identity politics, and the effort to forge alliances out of groups that experience oppression or injustice in different ways.[6]

On the one hand, identity politics seems to be a destructive solvent of all efforts to achieve political solidarity; even the famous universal solvent. This is the argument made by, for example, Todd Gitlin, in his recent *Twilight of Common Dreams.*[7] The "common dream" Gitlin's most concerned with is the Left's dream of democratic socialism (a term that as amended by feminist understandings might easily be attached to the philosophy I've outlined in this book). His contention is that the dream has become unrealizable, chiefly because the social groups that might be its constituents are too narcissistically focused on their own oppressions to form effective political alliances with each other; and especially with, he clearly implies, those white men (and often white women) without whose support there can be no effective mass movement. In the spring and summer of 1997 Gitlin's fears achieved the status of journalistic recognition when the white "Left" representative in the New York City mayoral race, Ruth Messinger, was forced to choose between two would-be candidates (among others) for Manhattan borough president on the Democratic ticket, one a black woman and the other a gay woman; and the supporters of each made it perfectly clear that there would be no forgiveness once she made, as she inevitably had to make, the "wrong" endorsement.

Clearly Gitlin is correct that a mass egalitarian movement is unattainable in the face of this kind of identity politics. It is equally clear, although here Gitlin is reluctant to acknowledge the obvious, that identity politics is a historically generated movement (or series of movements) that responds quite accurately, *in the short run,* to the circumstances of a fractured polity. The working class has decomposed (not just in the United States but in almost all contemporary capitalist societies) in the face of rapid technological change and the internationalization of competition. Consequently even reformist (let alone revolutionary) labor movement politics has clearly become the politics of considerably less than half the people as well as being ill-attuned to the real problems of globalization.

In these circumstances, those persons who understand themselves as oppressed by the majority in a democratic society, if they seek formal political relief at all, often turn to liberal institutions of constitutional protection rather than to mass democratic institutions of political party mobilization. If they are too oppressed or alienated even to see the legal system as a possible protector, they turn back on themselves—the only group they can trust.

In the United States, however, where the politics of group self-defense has advanced farther than almost anywhere else (the former Yugoslavia, India, and Rwanda being signal exceptions to that generalization), the official ideology of liberal constitutionalism *demands* the assertion of identity in order to merit its protection.[8] For example, the American Supreme Court has ruled that "race" is a suspect category, in that anything that looks like racial discrimination must pass the highest level of judicial scrutiny. For those who practice discrimination, judicial scrutiny is also a lot more threatening than its always reluctant legislative counterpart; it is hard for the victims of discrimination not to be aware of this.[9]

In order for a particular *individual* in the United States to merit this judicial protection, however, he or she must be seen as belonging to the protected category; and this becomes yet one more compelling reason to embrace what may already be strongly felt group identities. Just as, in Sartre's famous phrase, a Jew is anyone society treats as a Jew, so an African American, for example, becomes anyone society treats as such; both for worse and for better. So "race," the most destructively divisive category in human social history and one of the most conceptually and scientifically fraudulent, first becomes hypostasized as though it were a concrete reality, and then, disastrously, actually becomes a concrete reality.

As with race, so with ethnic origin or nationality, sexuality, gender: not through some conspiracy of liberal elites or the irrational stubborness of the excluded and marginalized but through the normal, expectable operations of political institutions. The condition of minorities asserting their identities is simply that they do not have, or reasonably do not think they have, any other chance of obtaining fair treatment from a majority that has never treated them as equals. In the absence of a mass movement such as Roosevelt's New Deal coalition or the European Communist and Socialist parties, a movement able to persuade its constituent parts that it represents the historical needs of everyone, they have no other alternative. The most successful of these and the model for all mass reformist movements, Swedish social democracy in its heyday, was rooted in a national labor federation (the L.O.) that represented almost the entire nonrural work force. This now seems to belong in a distant, almost utopian, past (even in relatively homogeneous Sweden).

Identity politics, in other words, is not the *cause* of the disappearance of mass mobilizing politics, but is rather one of its most devastating effects. The dilemma of the Left—Ruth Messinger's dilemma—is insoluble because it has no mass constituency for its would-be elements to be a part of. The solution to that dilemma is simple in principle, but impossible to will into existence in practice. A movement must come into being that is founded on egalitarian solidarity, a movement that mobilizes as equal members all those constituent elements. And yet, it can only come into being if they are prepared to be mobilized by it. Which must happen first, however, is a question that cannot be answered. Instead, egalitarians wherever they find themselves have to ask themselves what it means to practice solidarity in the search for more equality without worrying about how to generate it by probably impossible acts of will. If we can't or won't do that much, then the search will be fruitless.

What ought mutual recognition and empathy to mean, then, from the standpoint either of those who like Gitlin (and myself) still adhere to universalistic principles of political action, or of those practitioners of identity politics whom he criticizes? The answer to this question is two-sided.

On the one hand, universalistic principles ("justice," "fairness," "equality," etc.) are empty verbiage until and unless they find concrete application in an understanding of the different kinds of lives that people live and the different ways in which personality can manifest itself. If I can't recognize particular forms of injustice to others, then I cannot claim to be able to recognize it at all. To return to an earlier example, the law of "self-defense" is *not* truly universal when stated as an invariant requirement that the defender who invokes it must have been in immediate danger of her life, must not have been able to escape, and must have had no other recourse to save her life except to kill the person against whom she was defending herself. Here, because of the historical and cultural conditioning as well as, for many, the biological reality that makes women's resort to violence so much more of a last resort than men's; and because not only for that reason but for many others women very often find it extremely difficult to simply leave the men with whom they live (which, for example, might also require leaving children at their mercy), the invocation of formal legal rules is a travesty of fairness and equal treatment. But it is a proper understanding of those universal principles, not repudiation of them, that exposes the travesty and compels us to try to change the law itself.

The true task of the self-styled universalist is to listen to accounts of the history with which he or she is unfamiliar and, *more crucially*, to enlarge his or her previous vision of what constitutes the bedrock issues of egalitarian politics. The male leftists who throw up their hands in despair when a female colleague announces uncompromisingly that the right to abortion is the bedrock issue for egalitarians are doing much more damage to any putative egalitarian movement than she is.[10]It's not that she's necessarily right about her priority (only history will decide that) or that one can't claim to be both opposed to abortion rights and a "real" egalitarian. What is unquestionable, rather, is that her statement stems from a reasoned, historically informed assessment linking gendered conditions and practices (e.g., men don't get pregnant and find it much easier to escape the various consequences of child-bearing) to the real prospects of equal opportunity for concrete female persons. This is a theory of linkage that many feminists have been elaborating for more than two decades and that millions of women have been "voting for" with their bodies. Not to know this, not to understand the linkage at least well enough to be able politely to argue with it on its own terms, is not to have been listening.

In the same way, it requires an extraordinary failure of attention not to know that much of the time urban police forces in the United States appear to many African Ameri-

cans, quite reasonably, as a sometimes brutal and often uncaring occupying army; and that this relationship is again
less the consequence of the "law and order" problem than its
continuing cause. How can there be a commitment to "law
and order" when its official representatives are constantly
observed to be unlawful and disorderly? Or, to revert to a
previous example, when middle class African-Americans,
male or female, know that they can not walk through department stores without being trailed by store detectives or
floorwalkers; and when in large cities even African American detectives walk in fear of being "mistaken" for criminals by their colleagues? To be always and everywhere one
of the usual suspects marks one's entire life; it is a different
life, and apparently self-centered theories of "difference"
become, whatever else they are, no less than accurately de-
scriptive of that life.

This is even more evident when we encounter the justifications for discriminatory treatment, which is that some
unspecified but particularly large proportion of African
Americans in fact does commit crimes of street violence, or
shoplift in department stores. The truth or falsity of these
justifications doesn't matter. To treat individuals as though
they are nothing but representatives of stereotypes is what
we mean by "discrimination." What this does is to rein-
scribe the practices of racial discrimination that were and to
this extent still are the daily face of white supremacism. As
a practice of self-defense—the maintenance of a threatened
privilege—white supremacism can of course be justified.
But not as a practice of egalitarianism.[11] It is the politics of
force rather than of equality.

This particular understanding is thus based on the kind of
recognition of another's circumstances that we call "empathy." We who have never been in this particular instance of

what feels to the person in it like an inescapable trap, imaginatively put ourselves in that person's place and try to appreciate her situation from her point of view. Men, for example, have to *recognize* the femaleness of being female; recognize it not as a "condition" in the sense of a dread disease but as a structured social condition that is fundamentally different and in some instances fundamentally more dangerous than their own. At the same time, however, these same reflective men have to recognize that there are different ways of being male, some of which—being gay, for example—may be every bit as "different" and dangerous as being anatomically and socially "female." This particular process of understanding leads to the recognition that there is such a thing as, say, a socially meaningful class of gay men in general, distinct from women in general but similar to each other in being also distinct from men in general taken as normatively "masculine."

In this way the putative process of coalition formation advances; the number of people who understand themselves as having what I've called permanently common but in some way endangered human interests and who are thus prepared to demand equal opportunity in concert with other people's similar demands grows decisively. Unfortunately, it is precisely this kind of empathy that is missing from the approach that many universalistic white leftists, such as Gitlin in *The Twilight of Common Dreams*, consistently take toward those who respond to a different history in a different voice. When "difference" visibly comes to mean "other," empathy disappears; and dialogue stops.

Obviously dialogue cannot always end in agreement; that would have no credibility and would be a waste of everyone's time. But however dialogue is to proceed, there is a serious problem with traditional, universalistic appeals to solidarity such as Gitlin's. The problem is evident in Gitlin's title, "The Twilight of *Common Dreams*" (my emphasis). To speak, whether in mourning or in celebration, the language of commonality, is to imply that one knows what the common language is, and what "dreams" (including presumably moral and political dreams) it entails. But this is precisely what we don't know and can't imply. If I think back to the "common dreams" of the socialist movement at its height, for example, these are among the many "dreams" that its leaders did *not* consider part of its common moral language: the dream that every woman has the right to control her own body; the dream that choice of sexual partners is a rightfully important aspect of one's human identity; even the fully racially integrative "dream" of Martin Luther King Jr.

What is even more problematic than overstating the commonality of the common is what usually follows the correction of that overstatement; that is, an amendment of the speaker's notion of solidarity to include those who were previously excluded. The amendment process unfortunately is even more problematic, in that by virtue of those previous exclusions the common language was not truly common. To think that we can best proceed by amending it is still to privilege its authors (traditional Marxists and liberals, usually) as authoritative. "We" begin where "they" benignly left off; their vision was incomplete but otherwise unobjectionable. As Jodi Dean writes in her book *Solidarity of Strangers*, "liberal tolerance seems to adopt a just-add-it-on perspective toward inclusion . . ." One typical outcome of this approach, for example, is that "by denying our responsibility to displace those crystallizations of meaning constructing women and homosexuals as 'other,' it fails to examine the oppositional and exclusionary interpretations of rights as they have become embedded in our legal system."[12] As long as our own claims to authority and our own failures of self-examination go unnoticed by spokespersons for an egalitarian movement yet to be, there will be no such movement.

Thus on the one hand, after reading not only Gitlin's critical account of the Oakland school board's debate about adopting "Ebonics" as a primary language skill (the account with which he begins his critique of "identity politics") as well as the contrary accounts of those who support the board's decision to do so, I have come to the considered judgment that he has a good point. The kind of cultural nationalism lying behind the board's decision-making process, even though it responded to a real need, was a pedagogical and political disaster in the making. However, this is not because it represented a separatist, segregationist deviation from a universalistic standard of liberal tolerance that once was and is now being betrayed.[13] Rather, the fight for "Ebonics" represented a separatist, segregationist, obstacle to creating a universalist standard of solidarity in mutual recognition *that is yet to be*.[14]

The italicized phrase tells us where we must begin the search for a workable universalism. The essential first step in generating the universalistic spirit of solidarity consists in a twofold recognition on the part of its *soi-disant* spokespersons. First, no one ever had or yet does have a legitimate monopoly in knowing how to separate true universality from its impersonations; classical philosophies of solidarity—*fraternite*, for example—were always only partial at best.[15] Second, the universalistic spirit of solidarity in its next incarnation, whatever it may turn out to be, will only come into existence out of the experiences of those people who have been excluded from its earlier representations;

who have been positioned as "other" and thus have had to struggle against the weight of structured inequality.

As I've argued at the end of chapter 7, these include feminists who, drawing upon their unique experience of being oppressed and yet necessarily living in intimacy with the oppressor, understand both the necessity of female solidarity and the equal necessity of transcending it. In the United States they include also African American theorists, Latino American theorists, "queer theorists," and others who can argue powerfully for a transnational solidarity. This is so precisely because these theorists have experienced the ambiguous but real attractions of the nationalist sentiment and of unforgiving rage at being constantly an object of exclusion, oppression, or contempt. Unlike most members of the white Left, they understand not only the necessity of transcending cultural particularism, but also why it is genuinely unavoidable in the first place.[16]

The universalistic spirit of solidarity, in other words, has to emanate from a truly universalist community, whether of activists or intellectuals. The inadequacy of Gitlin's, and my own, response to "Ebonics" is that we have never *needed* to speak another language; we have never felt *excluded* from the one we are supposed to speak; we have never felt *rage* at the depths of the need and the coldness of the exclusion. The understanding of that position is part of any allegedly universal ideal in action.

To be sure, this is so far the description only of a one-way process, consisting of nothing but the recognition by some people that others' lives are worse than theirs. It's the essential first step, but not the only one. No egalitarian politics ever was or ever will be constructed out of such a one-way process, which however necessary to it is not sufficient for it. Respect for others means treating them as equals, and equal treatment is always necessarily a *two-way* process. It is at this point that the requirements of a politics of solidarity, properly understood, do become incompatible with a certain kind of contemporary identity politics.

The root problem of the kinds of identity politics that are incompatible with the spirit of solidarity is that, as we've seen in my reference to resegregation, they take on the character of the politics of discrimination that inspired them in the first place. *What both deny is respect for individuals as such.* Egalitarianism does not demand the repudiation of felt group identities, but it does demand the repudiation of their moral primacy.

For example, "black power" as a slogan may have been a necessary inspiration to effectual political activity for some people; in the short run, the expulsion of non-black people from civil rights organizations it mandated may even have been an organizational necessity. In the same way, the slogan "black is beautiful" may have begun life as a necessary component of personality formation for many people in the United States. However, eventually and ineluctably, the two slogans taken together, and copied by many other marginalized or oppressed peoples as well—and, fatefully, even by people who can't be described in any such manner—have come to justify the resegregation of civil life.

At this point, "blackness" and "whiteness" take on the character of a willed opposition that denies the reality of the lives of millions of people who are neither "black" nor "white" in this prescriptive sense. "Black power," as a response to the implicit whiteness of legitimate power and authority, was historically the first moment of this movement; but the same thing happens, and is happening today, with all such polarities. Today American society is full of similar obstacles to the realization of a larger solidarity. Although hardly as central a support of inequality as the white complacency that gives it its sense of validity, black nationalism is one of these.

This is always the outcome of ethnic or cultural nationalism and of a politics based on them, whatever psychic benefits they might incidentally confer. This type of politics does call attention to experiences of injustice that others may not have previously recognized, and to that extent it performs a necessary function. But it does so at a heavy cost. Denying the full range of respect to others who are superficially not like the nationalist's self-image, and foregoing any impulse to empathize with *their* lives, it imposes stereotypes on individuals who were once not necessarily in opposition, but now are and must be; because they are no longer individuals with their own feelings, their own beliefs. Adopting the defining slogan of white racism as his own, the cultural nationalist asks plaintively, "How can you not want to be with your own people?"—a "people" thus reduced to nothing but the shading of a skin color, the intonation of a voice, or an anatomical description. That life is fuller for all of us when we live it among *different* people, all respecting and identifying with each other in that difference, becomes the thought that no one ever thinks. That is the life of multiculturalism properly understood; of cultural and social diversity; of a genuine pluralism.

That life, of cooperation with others of different experiences in seeking common goals, is also the only kind of life that will create the institutions of equal opportunity. In this context, the problem of group nationalism is not the difficulty it creates for excluded peoples in making common cause with persons such as myself or Todd Gitlin; to understand it in that way would be to trivialize it. The real difficulty with group nationalism—especially exclusivist group nationalism—is the obstacles it puts in the way of the excluded and oppressed who wish to build bridges *to each other*. To take one exemplary instance: in one Northeastern city with a large proportion of Spanish-speaking residents, the representatives of an organization devoted to improving the living condition of poor Latinos refuse to attend any conference with like-minded people unless the conference is held in Spanish. They don't want simultaneous translation from the English (the working language of most of the other likely participants in any coalition); they want Spanish to be the official language. But rather than putting up effective opposition to "English First" nativist intolerance, they have merely replicated its social divisiveness, for the conference has many African American representatives attending it as well, and their first language is English.

For many African Americans too linguistic exclusion has been a problem, but only in the more general sense that language has always been used by the privileged to separate themselves from those who lack privilege. Indeed, it has been a class and gendered phenomenon at least as much as a racial one. Failure to recognize what is held in common, as in this case, means that we can emphasize only that which divides us. Starting from a collection of such exclusivist nationalisms and nonnegotiable demands, the politics of equality quickly runs into the ground. Fighting each other replaces fighting together, and the already existing clash of material economic interests (for example, as we've seen, residents against immigrants) is accelerated.

Here then we have to distinguish between two kinds of "identity," only one of which leads in the direction of solidarity. In the most common contemporary usage, "identity" has come to mean the assertion of some special noteworthiness. "We" (and the "we" tends to be coercively inclusive) are meritorious because *some* of us are especially good at something, not because we all participate in a common humanity. Sandy Koufax was a great pitcher—and a Jew; Ralph Ellison is a great novelist—and black; Michelangelo was a great artist—and gay; Virginia Woolf was a great novelist—and a woman. This can all too unfortunately come to sound like its own version of the language of "Americanism": the exclusivist language of the Immigration Act of 1996, which divides the world into "us" and "them," the virtuous few and the alien others.

The antinomian version of identity plays itself out disastrously. It produces the stereotype of the person as always being one thing rather than another, as reducible to an identity constructed not by the struggles of achieving personhood but by some self- contradictory combination of biology and coercive social processes. It also easily produces a politics of victimization in which there is no sympathy for suffering in general, but only sympathy for the suffering of people who are exactly like oneself. At the same time it also produces the stereotype that all whites are "white" (or all men "male"), that as such they all benefit from a certain kind of privilege, and that none of them can understand what it is to be nonwhite (or female, etc.). Every one of those stereotypes is demonstrably false.

Much more insidious from an egalitarian perspective is the separatist solidarity that often follows from invocations of *fundamental* and ineradicable "difference." This version of solidarity can lead us into a moral and political cul-de-sac. Are gay men really more worthy of respect because Michelangelo was one of them? Does "black is beautiful" mean that the homeless black vet huddled in a doorway deserves a place to live because he is "beautiful"? If he was of what we consider mixed racial ancestry and did not call himself "black," would he be less deserving? On the contrary, he deserves whatever he deserves because he is a human being in need.

The dangerous temptation here is to confuse the strategic and political uses of nationalism, its capacity to inspire people to resist oppression and to demand self-government, with a moral theory that tells us who we are and why we deserve what we deserve. Nationalism cannot do that, and exclusivist nationalisms—the nationalisms of "identity"—least of all. Instead, when substituted for a moral theory of humanness, they tend to internalize the politics of contempt and then defiantly return it as a proclamation of the self. But the sole long-term result of this transaction is that contempt is further entrenched as the currency of political life. I must be something special, I must *belong*, to be deserving; and if I am not something special, if I do not belong, then I deserve nothing. The white liberals whose liberalism has turned to racial scorn (see Patricia Williams's anecdote above) now have more company than they deserve.[17]

Whatever their short-term historical justifications, exclusivist nationalisms ask the wrong question: who will respect my different way of life, or beliefs, or culture, instead of who will respect my equal human rights?[18] That latter question leads to the second way of asserting "identity." This, the politics of a what I've called a genuine multiculturalism, or pluralism, is totally different. It demands not so much that we discard stereotypes (after all, most of them would not have been developed if their distortions were not predicated on some observable condition), as that we recognize their irrelevance to reasoned or ethical behavior. They are irrelevant because I am whoever I am regardless of my social background; my identity is nothing more nor less than how I behave to others. If, as may be necessary on occasion, I assert pride in my identity, it is on the one hand because of my differences from you; but at the same time because of our fundamental similarity: we are both human.

The identity ascribed to a person and which that person may choose to embrace—her ethnicity, her religion, his language, his sexuality—is legitimately a source of pride only in this sense. First, it describes one way among many of being fully human. Second, it represents what for some people has been the special experience of struggle necessary to make others recognize that common humanity, which they have denied. But what makes all of us fully human is the fact that *they* are wrong. My full humanity, or yours, or anyone's, exists *regardless* of any particular identity. It inheres in the equal possibility we all have of living an ethical life: of being willing to work cooperatively for the benefit of others as well as one's own; of neither oppressing the weak nor toadying to the strong; and being always ready to recognize the common but differently inflected experiences of injustice.

The political salience of this kind of "identity," in contrast to that of identity politics, is indeed egalitarian. We empathize with the person who has been unjustly deprived of rights because that person is an individual and no individual should be unjustly deprived of rights; not because that person has one cultural identity rather than another. As to that, the real but limited usefulness of cultural group identities precisely depends on the extent to which they are reliable indicators that a person who claims to have suffered some deprivation probably has actually suffered it.

More concretely, to return to where we began this discus-

sion, when a *multitude* of persons with a shared social identity tell a common story about the frequency with which
they experience deprivation or injustice, that story demands
everyone else's attention. But the story is not worth any
more than its truth value in the light of reasoned discussion.
The supposed deprivation may not in fact exist. Neonazis are
not, as they claim they are, white people suffering from racial oppression; white people as white people have never suffered from racial oppression. They are merely white people
who have, because of various resentments, allowed themselves to become sociopaths. Alternatively, the supposed injustice may be entirely spurious. It is not unjust or unfair for
the children of biblical literalists to be exposed to the theory
of evolution, for otherwise they would be deprived of the
chance every human being ought to have: to encounter and
perhaps pursue scientific reasoning. In a democracy, educators should not willingly allow anyone to be so deprived.[19]

Thus the practitioners of an egalitarian politics of solidarity can never and should never promise that concrete *demands* consequent to the assertion of a group identity (e.g.,
adoption or rejection of a particular school curriculum;
specifications of priorities in a political program; communal
or educational segregation) will always be made good. If
that promise is kept, then the next step in this dance is that,
as in the United States, certain groups of whites who feel
themselves to be culturally outcast, will demand rejection of
a "multicultural" curriculum, insist on the teaching of cre-
ationism in place of biological science, and so forth. The
politics of oppressive censorship and coercive separatism is
firmly in place, and we are back in 1895—as though a century of egalitarianism had never happened.

What is missing in this movement is precisely what its

exemplars sometimes purport to stand for: a notion of *equality as a form of the good*. For a politics of equal opportunity the good is equal opportunity. As I've argued, mutual recognition is essential to the pursuit of this good. But mutual recognition is only a means to that good, and then only if the terms of mutual recognition are themselves egalitarian. Although mutual recognition is an absolute historical necessity, in its own terms it is value-less. It is compatible with any politics, even any oppression (some Nazis were at first more "Zionist" than most German Jews). Contrarily, egalitarianism is incompatible with many sincerely held political positions and certainly with any that justify oppression. For an egalitarian to be asked to give full respect to a "legitimate" cultural expression that is "incidentally" homophobic, misogynistic, separatist (and therefore segregationist), or contemptuous of others for stereotypical or meretricious reasons, is to be asked to do the impossible. Violent resistance to oppression is always in principle justifiable, even though it may or may not be justifiable in any particular instance. The oppression of others is *never* justifiable in any circumstances.

The problem with an unmitigated politics of identity, therefore, is that it turns a necessary and valid pride in oneself for being one kind of human being among many, into an excuse for behaviors that, in addition to being in no way justifiable, are in no way egalitarian. That those who are oppressive to others—say, men who abuse women—may themselves be oppressed in some other way, is an interesting fact for psychologists to theorize about, but no more than that. An explanation is not an excuse. The ultimate trajectory of this development is a self-defeating withdrawal from the only kind of collaborative politics that makes the pursuit of greater equality possible.

In sum, the sentiment of egalitarian solidarity is not merely a particular cultural expression like any other; nor is it a "perspective" reducible to some unique and "different" social position. It is an ineradicable and universal aspect of being human. The politics of equality proceeds from, and can only proceed from, that understanding.

NOTES

Introduction

1. Throughout I will be using the word "race" with quotation marks around it whenever the person thinking or speaking the term is myself. My own view is the consensual view of cultural and physical anthropologists: "race" is a purely ideological word that does not describe any significant genetic or physiological differences among peoples. For example, some people whose origins lie on the African continent have a somewhat different muscular structure and less susceptibility to sunburn than people of a European origin: that about sums up the so-called black–white racial difference. Given enough intermarriage, even these marginal and trivial differences would disappear. If we want to be accurate when talking about cultural differences based on social origins, we should ordinarily use the word *ethnicity*. That term merely describes places of origin; used properly, it has no connotations of innate difference and thus carries with it much less ideological or phantasmic baggage than does "race."

2. Jean-Jacques Rousseau, *On the Social Contract,* ed. by Roger D. Masters, trans. by Judith R. Masters (New York: St. Martin's Press, 1978), book 2, chapter 10, p. 75.

3. Ibid., p. 66.

4. On this point, see Michael Walzer, "Civil Disobedience and Corporate Authority," in Philip Green and Sanford Levinson, eds., *Power and Community: Dissenting Essays in Political Science* (New York: Pantheon Books, 1969), pp. 223–246. This essay is reprinted in Walzer's *Obligations: Essays on Disobedience, War, and Citizenship* (Cambridge: Harvard University Press, 1970), pp. 24–45. The late J. Anthony Lukas's *Big Trouble: A Murder in a Small Western Town Sets Off a Struggle for the Soul of America* (New York: Simon & Schuster, 1997) is a grand panoramic history of the class wars; that is, the war of capital against labor, and the latter's self- defense (though it would best be read in supplement to Louis Adamic's long out-of-print *Dynamite*). On the more recent period, see Rick Fantasia, *Cultures of Solidarity: Consciousness, Action, and Contemporary American Workers* (Berkeley: University of California Press, 1988).

5. *Capital,* Vol. 1 (London: Lawrence & Wishart, 1974), pp. 711–712. The

origins of capital are often well enough disguised to hide the bloodstains. Speaking of the "lending out of enormous amounts of capital" from England to the United States, Marx noted (p. 707) that "a great deal of capital, which appears today in the United States without any certificate of birth, was yesterday, in England, the capitalised blood of children." His entire discussion of the primitive accumulation that stands behind most of the great English fortunes appears as chapters. 26–33 of Volume One. The origins of American capital are more democratic, but often every bit as bloody.

6. For similar exercises at much greater and more detailed length, see Dworkin, "What is Equality? Part I: Equality of Welfare," *Philosophy and Public Affairs* 10 (summer 1981), pp. 185–246, and "What is Equality? Part II: Equality of Resources," *Philosophy and Public Affairs* 10 (fall 1981), pp. 283–345; and Bruce Ackerman, *Social Justice in the Liberal State* (New Haven: Yale University Press, 1980). Neither Dworkin or Ackerman makes John Locke's mistake of imagining a "New Found Land," North America, from which the indigenous inhabitants have been helpfully obliterated. For a more complete treatment of recent philosophical literature on equality, see Philip Green, "Equality Since Rawls: Objective Philosophers, Subjective Citizens, and Rational Choice," *Journal of Politics* (August 1985), pp. 970–97.

7. John Rawls, *A Theory of Justice* (Cambridge: Harvard University Press, 1971), especially chapter 3.

8. Milton Friedman, *Capitalism and Freedom* (Chicago: University of Chicago Press, 1962), p. 165.

9. William Letwin, "The Case Against Equality," in Letwin, ed., *Against Equality* (London: MacMillan, 1983), p. 8; and Peter T. Bauer, *Equality, the Third World, and Economic Delusion* (Cambridge: Harvard University Press, 1981), p. 17.

Chapter 2. Competing Principles

1. Karl Marx, *Critique of the Gotha Program*, English trans. (New York: International Publishers, 1938), p. 8.

2. Robert Nozick, *Anarchy, State, and Utopia* (New York: Basic Books, 1974), pp. 161–63. Chamberlain, a surly, unloved, and generally graceless seven-footer, is actually a poor example for Nozick. In his own right, other than helping his team to dominate, he did very little that anyone would pay to see compared to what Michael Jordan (or even Dennis Rodman) does. Nozick's misunderstanding of basketball is not a minor point, either; it suggests how careful we have to be, and how often we are simply wrong in thinking we know who deserves what.

3. The fetishism of commodities is the belief that the car has value because of its "carness," rather than because of the human labor that actually made it: "There it is a definite social relationship between men, that assumes, in their eyes, the fantastic form of a relationship between things." Karl Marx, *Capital*, vol. 1 (London: Lawrence and Wishart, 1974), p. 77. To the extent that the fetishism of commodities (as opposed to a straightforwardly sexual fetishism) does underlie our appreciation of a Tina Turner concert, say, it is what we might call a second-level, or derivative, commodity fetishism. It consists of our blindness to the multitudinous labor—of arrangers, sidemen, grips, electricians, security guards, etc.—that has made it possible for her to present herself to us as an apparently unmediated self.

4. Harry Braverman, *Labor and Monopoly Capital: The Degradation of Work in the Twentieth Century* (New York: Monthly Review Press, 1974), p. 413.

5. See Weber's "Politics as a Vocation," in H. H. Gerth and C. Wright Mills, eds., *From Max Weber: Essays in Sociology* (New York: Oxford University Press, 1958), p. 78. In *Anarchy, State, and Utopia* Nozick, the most unmitigatedly libertarian of contemporary political philosophers, puts the foundations of the minimal state as follows: property possessors in a "state of nature" (i.e., living together without the form of coercive political organization we call the state), come together and hire private protective agencies (where did *they* come from?) to protect their possessions; and the dominant protective agency becomes "the state" (see chapter 2). Weber, not to mention Rousseau, Marx, Lenin, and Trotsky (whom Weber was quoting), would surely feel vindicated by this scenario. If even a libertarian thinks that armed force is necessary to turn possession into ownership, who could possibly disagree?

6. In *Capital*, chapter 7, sec. 2.

7. Jean-Jacques Rousseau, "A Discourse on the Origin of Inequality," in *The Social Contract and Discourses,* trans. by G. D. H. Cole (New York: E. P. Dutton, 1950), pp. 196–97.

8. Emphasis added. See *Hegel's Philosophy of Right,* trans. by T. M. Knox (New York: Oxford University Press, 1952), p. 128 (paragraph 195).

9. Karl Marx, *Grundrisse: Introduction to the Critique of Political Economy,* trans. by Martin Nicolaus (Harmondsworth, Eng.: Penguin Books, 1973), pp. 275–89. Friedman, *Capitalism and Freedom* (Chicago: University of Chicago Press, 1962), p. 14; C. B. MacPherson, *Democratic Theory: Essays in Retrieval* (Oxford: Oxford University Press, 1963), p. 145 (emphases in original).

10. See Philip Green, "Prologomena to a Democratic Theory of the Division of Labor," *Philosophical Forum*, Vol. XIV, nos. 3–4, (spring–summer 1983), 263–95, for an extended analysis of this point; the quote is at 278–79. (Re-

produced as chapter 3 of *Retrieving Democracy: In Search of Civic Equality*,
Totowa, N.J.: Rowman and Allanheld, 1984). As Harry Braverman suc-
cinctly puts it, "The capitalist who hires servants is not making profits, but
spending them." Braverman, op. cit., p. 412.

11. Michael Young, *The Rise of the Meritocracy* (Harmondsworth, Eng.: Penguin Books, 1961).

12. Arthur Okun, *Equality and Efficiency: The Big Tradeoff* (Washington, D.C.:
The Brookings Institution, 1975), p. 85.

13. This is not true only of written tests. Almost all of these exercises exist for
the benefit of the people administering them, and to keep out new entrants.
A fireman may break weightlifting records and yet freeze in terror the first
time he has to carry a baby out of a burning building. In a lovely little study,
"Class, Culture, and the Persistence of an Elite: The Case of Army Officer
Selection" (*Sociological Review*, May 1978, pp. 283–304), Graeme Salaman
and Kenneth Thompson describe how candidate selection boards in Britain
used oral interviews to overturn the results of on-the- ground military exercises in which working-class candidates consistently did better than
upper-class ones. The former, it turns out, lacked "coolness under stress"; in
the post-exercise interviews they failed to keep a "stiff upper lip" when
describing their successes, whereas the upper-class twits were charmingly
modest about their lack of accomplishment.

14. When he was with the New York Yankees, Reggie Jackson was once asked
why his teammate Mickey Rivers, probably the faster runner in baseball,
dragged his feet so interminably when walking down to first base after receiving a free pass. Jackson replied that where Rivers came from (the streets
of Miami), he learned not to hurry because wherever you were going there
wasn't going to be anything worthwhile for you when you got there. This
was an exaggeration, of course, perhaps reflecting Jackson's own middle-
class bias as a successful and very well-assimilated graduate of the University of Arizona. It might have been more accurate to say (and most likely
what Jackson meant) that Rivers understood, as most people without that
experience do not, the necessity of husbanding your resources for when it
counts.

15. Consider, for example, the rebellion in many American state legislatures
against funding for "special educational needs."

16. In *Anarchy, State, and Utopia*, Nozick is able to derive a "minimal state"
from the voluntary acts of free people only because all his free actors are
men unencumbered by any social responsibility and concerned only with
their own property holdings. (As Susan Okin has noted, it is unclear whether
Nozick thinks that women and children should be thought of as men's property). It is a version of distributive justice for small boys, who haven't yet

encountered the messy social world, and still think that everything can be divided up into "mine" and "yours," "fair" and "unfair." See Susan Moller Okin, *Justice, Gender and the Family* (New York: Basic Books, 1989), pp. 74–88.

17. Conventional public discussion never touches on some of the profound ways in which an ideology of private property conjoined with a gendered division of labor produces and reproduces sexual inequality. The epidemic incestuous sexual exploitation of daughters by fathers (or father substitutes), for example, is enabled because "many men's privileged economic position means that families are often heavily dependent on the male wage . . . Mothers whose economic well-being depends on the presence of an incest-abusing father may create an atmosphere in which children rightly know that if they tell, it will be they and not their fathers who will be cast out of the family and despised . . . Even mothers who do believe their daughter's reports sometimes join the abusing fathers and urge the children to change their stories to protect the financial unity or life of the family." See Harriet Fraad, "At Home with Incest," *Rethinking Marxism*, vol. 9 no. 4 (winter 1996–97), pp. 16–39, 22.

18. For a complete list of what may not be for sale even in a capitalist society, see Michael Walzer's *Spheres of Justice* (New York: Basic Books, 1983), pp. 100–103. His list of "blocked exchanges" includes slavery, the buying of political office (?), criminal justice, basic rights and liberties, rights of marriage and procreation, the right of exit, exemption from military service, prizes and honors, divine grace, love and friendship, and various kinds of criminal sales (Murder, Inc.). He does not argue that none of these has ever been for sale (they all have at one time and place or another, including our own), but merely that "we," those who might be reading his book or mine, for example, can't in our own time and place reasonably argue for reinstating or formalizing as legitimate any of those blocked exchanges. There are in fact a handful of "rational choice" theorists and judges who will do so, but if their view were well known they would be thought by most people to be crazy. Even the kind of favor-giving that disfigures the American political process is possible only because of the opacity of American legislative institutions. It is not a "natural" outcome of governance, as any senator could discover by getting up in public and trying to explain why he was sneaking a hidden subsidy for his favorite corporation into the next omnibus appropriations bill.

19. Friedman, op. cit., pp. 23, 162.

20. See Nozick, op. cit., for this argument. Briefly, Nozick argues that once someone comes into possession of something by a legitimate method of ac-

quisition, all subsequent owners have a legitimate claim as long as the transfers along the chain of acquisition are neither by theft nor fraud.

21. For the best discussion of the way the subordination of women is inscribed in our conventional understandings of such liberal institutions as "the free market," "individual rights," etc., see Wendy Brown, *States of Injury: Power and Freedom in Late Modernity* (Princeton: Princeton University Press, 1995), chapter 6 ("Liberalism's Family Values").

Chapter 3. Equal Opportunity

1. See Stuart Hall, *The Hard Road to Renewal: Thatcherism and the Crisis of the Left* (New York: Verso, 1988), especially chapter 8, "Popular-Democratic vs. Authoritarian Populism: Two Ways of 'Taking Democracy Seriously.'"

2. See Michael Parenti, *Power and the Powerless* (New York: St. Martin's Press, 1978), pp. 67–72. *Power and the Powerless* is the best account of cumulative inequality available for the United States; although published two decades ago, it is "dated" only in the sense that the situation (for the poor and nonwhite, male and female) is much worse now than when Parenti first described it. For a good update see Sheila Collins, *Let Them Eat Ketchup! The Politics of Poverty and Inequality* (New York: Monthly Review Press, 1996).

3. See C. McCord and H. P. Freeman, "Excess Mortality in Harlem," *New England Journal of Medicine*; and Sen, *ibid.*, p. 115. All emphases in original.

4. The best brief discussion of this is Michael Walzer's "Exclusion, Injustice, and Democracy," *Dissent* Vol. 40 no. 1 (winter 1993), pp. 55–64. For a full-length treatment based on intensive interviews with people who have been excluded by public institutions and denigrated by public rhetoric, see Louise Armstrong, *Of 'Sluts' and bastards: a Feminist decodes the Child Welfare debate*, (Monroe, Me.: Common Courage Press, 1995).

5. The phrase made famous, of course, by William Ryan in his *Blaming the Victim* (New York: Pantheon Books, 1971).

6. See *Harris* v. *McRae*, 448 U.S. 297 (1980) 323. Stewart's majority opinion upheld the so-called Hyde Amendment, which proscribed Medicaid payments for abortion.

7. In a recent detective story called *High-Heel Blues* (New York: Simon and Schuster, 1997), by Diane K. Shah, the narrator-heroine is a policewoman whose husband, she discovers, is a cocaine addict. Her response is to compel him to enter the Betty Ford Clinic. Ms. Shah is co-author of ex–Los Angeles Police Chief Daryl Gates's "autobiography," and her acknowledgements include an enthusiastic endorsement both of Gates and of the LAPD in general. The narrator never even notices how out of tune her "treatment" ap-

proach to her husband is with her general approach to law-and-order where ordinary drug users are concerned.

8. Among the many sources on different welfare states and their policies, see especially Diane Sainsbury, ed., *Gendering Welfare States* (Thousand Oaks, Calif.: Sage Publications, 1994); and Linda Gordon, ed., *Women, the State, and Welfare* (Madison: University of Wisconsin Press, 1990). In the former collection, "Work, Welfare, and Gender Equality," an essay by Alan Siaroff uncovers a type of what he calls "Protestant social democratic welfare states" (really, the Scandinavian tier of Northern Europe), which "are the only nations to provide (comparatively) a true 'work-welfare choice' for women, in that female work as an end in itself is relatively desirable." (p. 95). The United States belongs to the group he calls "Protestant liberal welfare states," or nations with "minimal family welfare yet a relatively egalitarian gender situation in the labour market."

9. The apparent reference to Ben Barber's "strong democracy" is not unintended; see Barber's *Strong Democracy* (Berkeley: University of California Press, 1984).

10. All these requirements taken together are equivalent to what Amartya K. Sen calls "capability": "a set of vectors or functionings, reflecting the person's freedom to lead one type of life or another"; or, "primarily a reflection of the freedom to achieve valuable functionings." See Amartya K. Sen, *Inequality Reexamined* (Cambridge: Harvard University Press, 1992), pp. 40, 49. "Valuable" here means, of course, valuable by some relevant standards—i.e., these are different in the United States than in India. On the other hand, they may not be entirely unrelated. Since the United States has more of an impact on life in India than vice versa, Indians may feel justified in making certain egalitarian demands on the United States—in, e.g., the terms of trade. See chapter 7.

11. Here I implicitly follow John Rawls (*A Theory of Justice*, op.cit.; see pp. 223 ff. below), who assigns first priority to the principle of equal political liberty and second priority to the difference principle (social or economic inequalities are justified only if they favor the least advantaged).

12. For a much fuller discussion, see my *Retrieving Democracy: In Search of Civic Equality* (Totowa, N.J.: Rowman and Allanheld, 1985).

13. E. E. Schattschneider, *The Semi-Sovereign People* (New York: Holt, Rinehart and Winston, 1960), p. 141 (italics his).

14. For a summary of how overwhelmingly the mass media marginalize and exclude nonwhite persons from the world of "information," see Christopher P. Campbell, *Race, Myth, and the News* (Thousand Oaks, Calif.: Sage Publications, 1995). On how the world of propaganda masquerades as "news" in the ventriloquist's voices of stuffed shirts in blue suits, see Edward S. Her-

man and Noam Chomsky, *Manufacturing Consent: The Political Economy of the Mass Media* (New York: Pantheon Books, 1988). For an elaboration of the importance of media control in an age of images, see my comments in Philip Green, ed., *Democracy* (Atlantic Highlands, N.J.: Humanities Press, 1993), pp. 164–67.

15. The best example of compensatory access to the mass media is Britain's Channel 4, which, for all its limitations in practice, was established by Parliament to give special representation to "minority voices" on the television spectrum. The most noteworthy point about Channel 4 is that it is supported not, as is the American Public Broadcasting System, by a subsidy that can at any moment be reduced or withdrawn, but by a levy (10 percent) on the gross proceeds of the commercial channels. So the more successful is conventional mass television, the more it benefits unconventional alternatives. This is the exact opposite of how the American "free market" in television works; see Philip Green, "American Television and Consumer Democracy," *Dissent* vol. 45, no. 2 (spring 1998), 49–57.

16. The most useful discussions of how to amplify the voices of the excluded and marginalized are Iris Marion Young, *Justice and the Politics of Difference* (Princeton: Princeton University Press, 1990); Lani Guinier, *Tyranny of the Majority: Fundamental Fairness in Representative Democracy* (New York: The Free Press, 1994); and Anne Phillips, *Engendering Democracy* (Harrisburg: Penn State University Press, 1991), especially chapter 5, from which the quotation about "domestic commitments" (by two members of the Icelandic Women's Party) is taken (p. 139).

17. Christian Bay, in the Introduction to his *Structure of Freedom* (Palo Alto: Stanford University Press, 1958; rev. ed., New York: Atheneum Press, 1965).

18. The simplest first step to take in order to limit private campaign spending would be to require television networks—which are, after all, public licensees having monopolistic use of a public resource—to provide a limited amount of free advertising time to candidates for political office and to forbid them from selling any further amounts of time.

Chapter 4. Achieving Equality

1. Thus Nozick's version of contractarianism, in which property holders hire a protective agency that gradually becomes a dominant protective agency and then a state, is for unequals only. If everyone were a property holder with roughly equal amounts held individually, a state would certainly still come into existence; but the egalitarian and welfarist considerations I have outlined here would be at least as compelling as the universal desire to protect private property against theft.

2. John Stuart Mill, *Utilitarianism* (Indianapolis: Hackett Publishing Company, 1979), p. 31. We do not have to take Mill's seemingly benign view of all "people" literally to grasp his point.

3. This argument is somewhat different from that made by John Rawls in defense of his second principle of justice ("the difference principle"), according to which "social and economic inequalities are to be arranged so that they are both (a) reasonably expected to be to everyone's advantage; and (b) attached to positions and offices open to all." (*A Theory of Justice*, op.cit. p. 60). According to Rawls, the principles of justice are those we would choose from a position of "reflective equilibrium," which is similar to what I have called "reasoned consideration" (see p. 38 above). The difference principle itself, however, is based primarily on a notion of risk aversion, according to which people would choose it because, operating behind a "veil of ignorance," they would realize that they might turn out to be among "the least advantaged." This looks much less like a "reflective equilibrium" than it looks like a standard welfare economics equilibrium, arrived at by individual actors pursuing their own utilities under conditions of uncertainty. What is therefore missing from Rawls's justification is any feeling of conscious cooperation among people trying not only to "deal with" each other, but to work together for what they recognize as common human goals of freedom, rights, and equality.

4. See the remarks of Sen, op. cit., p. 3.

5. For a full-length exposition of the necessity of starting moral reasoning about politics from the assumption of a capitalist social order, see Richard W. Miller, *Moral Differences: Truth, Justice, and Conscience in a World of Conflict* (Princeton: Princeton University Press, 1992). Miller, by profession a moral philosopher, argues less from the necessities of political economy (although he does that as well) and more from the exigencies of a human, moral diversity too extensive to be expressed in or captured by any centralized schema such as a "planned economy," a controlled labor market, etc.

6. The intellectual and scholarly fraudulence of racial genetics, especially, has been established over and over again; see, for example, Stephen J. Gould, *The Mismeasure of Man* (New York: W. W. Norton, 1981); Richard C. Lewontin, Steven Rose, and Leon J. Kamin, *Not In Our Genes* (New York: Pantheon Books, 1984); Philip Green, *The Pursuit of Inequality* (New York: Pantheon Books, 1981); Russell Jacoby and Naomi Glauberman, eds., *The Bell Curve Debate: History, Documents, Opinions* (New York: Random House, 1995); and Claude S. Fischer et al. *Inequality by Design: Cracking the Bell Curve Myth* (Princeton: Princeton University Press, 1996). This list only scratches the surface. The refutations accomplish little, however. The fanatics and obsessives of IQ and race proceed simply by ignoring all criti-

cisms and endlessly recycling the same worthless, refuted "data" over and over again (telling us, for example, that early childhood education, such as the Head Start program, can't increase cognitive abilities). Because they are politically important and have been coddled by respectable opinion outlets (*Harvard Education Review, The New York Times Book Review,* The Free Press) they are often taken seriously even by those who know something is wrong but don't have the expertise or energy to track down thousands of so-called scholarly footnotes; and so the dance continues. Thus it never gets said out loud that this "scholarship" is only slightly above the level of that of "the Holocaust never happened" school or the explorers of alien abductions.

7. For an elaboration of the dynamics of this vicious circle, see Edmund S. Phelps, *Rewarding Work: How to Restore Participation and Self-Support to Free Enterprise* (Cambridge: Harvard University Press, 1997).

8. My term, "surplus inequality," deliberately conjures up Herbert Marcuse's adaptation of Freud in the phrase, "surplus repression: the restrictions necessitated by social domination . . . distinguished from (basic) *repression*: the 'modifications' of the instincts necessary for the perpetuation of the human race in civilization." See his *Eros and Civilization: A Philosophical Inquiry into Freud* (Boston: Beacon Press, 1955), p. 32. It also has much in common with the "analytical Marxist" economist John Roemer's discussion of exploitation, in which he argues that the working class in capitalist society can be considered "exploited" only if its members would be contingently better off under some feasible alternative organization of the means of production; see his *General Theory of Exploitation and Class* (Cambridge, Mass.: Harvard University Press, 1982). All these formulas have their roots in Marx's distinction between "surplus labor in general, as labour performed over and above the given requirements [that] must always remain," and surplus-labour that in capitalist and slave societies "merely assumes an antagonistic form and is supplemented by complete idleness of a stratum of society." See *Capital,* vol. 3 (London: Lawrence and Wishart, 1972), p. 819.

9. I in no way mean to imply agreement with the conservative lie that welfare creates dependency, whereas work instills the spirit of independence. Welfare without any future of work indeed breeds hopelessness, but so does work at below-subsistence wages under conditions of exploitation and often brutality. And the latter may be much more debilitating to both women and children. In any event, most clients of the welfare system have typically moved in and out of what is recognized as gainful employment; those who can plausibly be characterized as belonging to a permanent class of dependents emotionally scarred by their dependency have never been more than

a marginal proportion of the total. See, e.g., Sanford Schram's *Words of Welfare: The Poverty of Social Science and the Social Science of Poverty* (Minneapolis: University of Minnesota Press, 1995), chapter 2.

10. For a description of the Swedish system at its peak, see Henry Milner, *Sweden: Social Democracy in Practice* (New York: Oxford Unviersity Press, 1990), chapter 7. American readers might be startled to learn of the services that are provided for free or for a small fee that anyone can afford (although there has been some slippage in recent years): for example, birth control needs, alcohol and drug counseling, dental services for children, and prescription drugs. So comprehensive is coverage that, as Milner puts it (p. 191), "average household income for the severely handicapped [is] only slightly below that of households without handicapped members . . ."

11. Sen, *Inequality Reexamined,* p. 109.

12. See "How Federal Budget Decisions Affect Us All," *America at a Glance* (Northampton, MA.: The National Priorities Project, 1997).

13. On the kinds of claims that the welfare state has answered to in the past and might have to answer to differently in the future, see Linda Gordon, ed., *Women, the State, and Welfare* (Madison: University of Wisconsin Press, 1990); and especially Nancy Fraser's "Struggle Over Needs: Outline of a Socialist-Feminist Critical Theory of Late-Capitalist Political Culture" (pp. 199–225). Fraser's essay is also available as chapter 8 of her *Unruly Practices: Power, Discourse, and Gender in Contemporary Social Theory* (Minneapolis: University of Minnesota Press, 1989). It originally appeared, in slightly different form, in *Ethics,* vol. 99 no. 2 (January 1989). This essay is fundamental to any present version of "socialist feminism"—the rubric under which I would place theories of equality such as my own.

14. See Shirley P. Burggraf, *The Feminine Economy and Economic Man: Reviving the Role of Family in the Post-Industrial Age* (New York: Addison-Wesley, 1997). There are contemporary societies where efforts are made to reward motherhood (France and Canada, for example) or alternatively to divide up parenting more evenly (Sweden). Whether the treatment of motherhood is in fact sufficient in those societies is a separate question that can only be addressed in the light of some explicit (or at least implicit) egalitarian standard. American women would be fortunate even to be able to begin that debate. It can be said, of course, that paying mothers to be mothers necessarily raises the likelihood of divorce to unacceptable levels. It could also be said, in reply, that in the long run that need not happen if men become better partners. For a consideration of these issues see *Retrieving Democracy,* op.cit., pp. 96–108.

15. See chapter 5. The most graphic contemporary examples of discrimination usually have to do with pregnancy. For example, more and more in the United States women who smoke and drink while pregnant are being

treated as criminals: the revenge of the antiabortion movement. But fathers who smoke and drink also can potentially pass on genetic defects to their children. The only difference is that they do it earlier in the chain of transmission (before, one might say, they were certain they were going to be fathers), and it would therefore require some general kind of prohibition to constrain their behavior. To punish women because it's easier to quarantine their behavior is like punishing drug users because they're easier to catch than drug suppliers: it repudiates the principle of equal justice on behalf of a purely suppositional and discriminatory notion of social utility. See Cynthia R. Daniels, "Between Fathers and Fetuses: The Social Construction of Male Reproduction and the Politics of Fetal Harm," *Signs: Journal of Women in Culture and Society* vol. 22 no. 3 (spring 1997), pp. 579–616; and more generally, her *At Women's Expense: State Power and the Politics of Fetal Rights* (Cambridge: Harvard University Press, 1993).

16. The classic discussion of this issue is Karl Polanyi's explanation of the nineteenth-century abolition of the poor law in Great Britain, in his *The Great Transformation* (New York: Rinehart and Company, 1944), chapter 7.

17. Nothing any egalitarian can say will eradicate the propensity among some people to be lazy, lawless, or to revel in their own lack of competence. There's no point, therefore, in imagining either types of social service that sop up the efforts (or lack of effort) of such people, or elaborate psychological theories that explain how they'd all really disappear in a better society. The only point about an egalitarian society is that it shouldn't be any easier for people to goof off because they've inherited a living.

18. Cf. Arlie Russell Hochschild, *The Time Bind: When Work Becomes Home and Home Becomes Work* (New York: Metropolitan Books, 1997). As Hochschild's title suggests, her argument is that the attraction of being "at work" is a measure of the unattractiveness, for women as well as men, of being at home. It seems clear (see above) what combination of policies would make home more attractive to women. How to make home more attractive to men is less clear, but the provision of economic and job security at European rather than American levels would seem to be part of the answer. European workers typically behave as though the more leisure time the better, where Americans often are chafing by the end of their comparatively briefer vacations from work.

19. Once again, the unsurpassed story of human reaction to the ravages of the free labor market is Polanyi's *The Great Transformation*.

Chapter 5. The Costs of Equality

1. See Edward N. Wolff, *Top Heavy: The Increasing Inequality of Wealth in the United States and What Can Be Done about It* (New York: The New Press, 1995), pp. 10–11.

2. See Okun, op. cit.

3. I have phrased the comparison as a sort of double negative despite the grammatical ungainliness that results, because none of the societies being compared could actually be called a society of equals; it's just that some are less unequal than others. The technical economic literature on this subject is summed up and discussed by Samuel Bowles and Herbert Gintis, in "Efficient Redistribution: New Rules for Markets, States, and Communities," *Politics and Society* vol. 24 no. 4 (December 1996), pp. 307–42. The technical argument in its most abstruse theoretical form, but with supportive empirical/historical material, is contained in several "working papers" from the National Bureau of Economic Research, including Torsten Persson and Guido Tabellini, "Is Inequality Harmful for Growth? Theory and Evidence," working paper no.3599; Roland Benabou, "Unequal Societies," working paper no. 5583; and Benabou, "Inequality and Growth," working paper no. 5658.

4. On wealth taxes and how they have worked in several European democracies, see Wolff's *Top Heavy*, especially chapters 7 and 8. Wolff's simulation for the United States of the effects of a Swedish-type, highly progressive wealth tax on stock shares, bonds, and luxury household goods (e.g., jewelry, boats), shows that it would reduce inequality as much as the personal income tax (p. 50). On "the maximum wage," see *The Maximum Wage: A Common-Sense Prescription for Revitalizing America — By Taxing the Very Rich*, by Sam Pizzigati (New York: Apex Press, 1992). Pizzigati's specific proposal, a "ten times the minimum wage" maximum, is certainly unworkable for the reasons advanced above.

5. For an extensive consideration of this argument, see Bowles and Gintis, op. cit.

6. The best recent defense of the human moral imagination is Kristen Renwick Monroe's *The Heart of Altruism: Perceptions of a Common Humanity* (Princeton: Princeton University Press, 1996).

7. For example, two players might have a secret understanding, much like baseball signals (hand to arm, hand to forehead, etc.) that a certain gesture means, say, a void in one suit (e.g., no spades).

8. See Michael Novak, *The Spirit of Democratic Capitalism* (New York: Simon and Schuster, 1982), pp. 203–4. I do not mean to imply that Novak is a closet egalitarian. His work demonstrates no respect at all for those with "unequal" talents and he doesn't subject capitalism to any serious ethical inquiry.

9. It is not unfair to note that some later-generation Rockefellers, such as Nelson, had much more ability at spending money than at making it.

10. For one such story of the kind of inventor whose obsessive pursuit of his vision changed the world, and who expected nothing more than a one-time

monetary prize for his efforts, see Dava Sobel, *Longitude: The True Story of a Lone Scientific Genius Who Solved the Greatest Scientific Problem of His Time* (New York: Walker, 1995).

11. See *Capital*, op. cit., part 2, chapter 6, p. 172.

12. Economists sometimes promote confusion here by telling the rest of us that the "income" of such giants of personal wealth as Sam Walton is in some sense legitimated by the apparent utility to consumers of buying at Wal-Mart. However, none of us engaged in purchasing a good makes any explicit or implicit judgment on the way in which our payment is distributed afterwards. We do want the goods, but we have no idea whether cutting Walton's yearly appropriation tenfold or a hundred fold and increasing the take-home pay of cashiers and other service staff would have any effect on overall production or price. Here Robert Nozick's "Wilt Chamberlain" parable (see p. 18 above) is useful. Would any of us put several dollars from the price of a microwave, say, into a box marked "Sam"? I doubt that any reader's reaction to that question would be different from my own.

13. On the poor fit between credentials and job requirements or on-the-job performance, see, explicitly, Andrew Hacker, *Money: Who Has How Much and Why* (New York: Scribner, 1997), chapter 11 ; and inferentially, Peter Gottschalk, "Inequality, Income Growth, and Mobility: The Basic Facts," *The Journal of Economic Perspectives* vol. 22 no. 2 (spring 1997), pp. 21–40. And see especially *Inequality by Design* (op. cit., n. 6 above), especially chapters 7 and 9, for definitive evidence about the flexibility of "intelligence."

Chapter 6. The Problem of Compensation

1. This discussion of discrimination and its abolition is abstract in one important sense. I have not made any comment here about the contemporary debate over equal treatment versus the recognition of "difference." Should Muslims in a largely Christian society be allowed to segregate girls into single-sex schools? Should women in dangerous workplaces be treated just as though they were men, or as though they are women who need special treatment in order recognize (and valorize) their difference from men? There is an extensive literature about such questions. From a jurisprudentialist standpoint, the debate is perhaps best represented in Katharine T. Bartlett and Rosanne Kennedy, eds., *Feminist Legal Theory: Readings in Law and Gender* (Boulder, Colo.: Westview Press, 1991); for a more general theoretical overview, see Anne Phillips, *Engendering Democracy* (University Park, Pa.: Penn State University Press, 1991); and also her *Democracy and Difference* (University Park: Penn State University Press, 1993). However, my own view about the competing principles underlying this debate is

that they cannot be resolved in a society where the majority respects neither equality *nor* difference, for in that context neither sheer egalitarianism nor the formal recognition of difference is satisfactory. Thus to insist uncompromisingly on either of the alternative resolutions is to retreat to dogma or fanaticism. On the other hand, in a social order where the majority was truly committed to egalitarianism, and thus respected difference as variety among equals or putative equals, the discussion would turn out to be the much less rancorous one of choosing the most effective tactic to an agreed-on end.

2. For a brief but definitive account, see Douglas S. Massey and Nancy A. Denton, *American Apartheid: Segregation and the Making of the Underclass* (Cambridge: Harvard University Press, 1993).

3. My comments here are limited to the racial pattern of development. Suburbanization also created a gentrified "noose" around the cities that excluded poorer whites as firmly as the white noose excluded nonwhites. See the essays in William K. Tabb and Larry Sawyers, eds., *Marxism and the Metropolis: New Perspectives in Urban Political Economy* (New York: Oxford University Press, 1978), for example.

4. See Parenti's account quoted in chapter 3.

5. *On the Social Contract,* op. cit., book 2, chapter 4, p. 62. The emphasis is mine.

6. *Plessy v. Ferguson, 163 U.S. 537 (1896).*

7. The "I" here is personal as well as metaphorical. I, Philip Green, the author of these pages, have indeed internalized all sorts of casual biases over years of living in a social order constructed around various sentiments of bias; and I must constantly make myself aware of this truth. The resultant phenomenon of "bending over backwards" must occasionally seem embarrassing or silly, but it is far preferable to its thoughtless alternative.

8. Thomas Sowell, during a debate on the Boston public television program *The Advocates,* January 26, 1978. Transcripts of the program can be obtained from WGBH Boston.

9. Sowell, of course, is himself an African American. But we should not forget that there's a long history of well-established black leaders, especially in the South, assuring anyone who might ask that their people "really wanted" to be segregated.

10. As an economist, has Thomas Sowell ever done anything, in theory or in practice, that contributed even one iota to the betterment of the world? The same question could be asked about me, of course, and you, the reader. But at least you and I are not making invidious remarks about other people's lack of eligibility and implicitly trumpeting our own.

11. *Who Gets Ahead? The Determinants of Economic Success in America,* by Christopher Jencks et al (New York: Basic Books, 1979), p. 121ff.

12. Popular culture obliquely expresses truths that are never said out loud. When Demi Moore snarls "suck my dick" at the climax of her hand-to-hand battle with the drill instructor in *G.I. Jane,* the irreducible masculinity of the military state—and what state is not military?—is laid clear. The best account of the masculinized state is R. W. Connell's *Gender and Power: Society, the Person and Sexual Politics* (Stanford: Stanford University Press, 1987).

13. It must seem odd that someone who has taught at an all-women's college for thirty-five years should be justifying "diversity" in the language I've used here. But this is like the paradox of color blindness all over again. The existence of all-women's schools, and also of "historically all-Negro" schools, is justified by the desire to secure diversity, that is, greater representation, within the larger society. Wellesley, Smith, Mt. Holyoke, and Barnard Colleges, for example, produce many more law students proportionately than do almost any other liberal arts college and most universities. Smith, the largest college for women, has for the past two decades ranked third among all colleges, behind Oberlin and (barely) Swarthmore in producing students who go on to earn doctorates. The quotation from Mill that follows says much about the need for these schools.

14. John Stuart Mill, *Utilitarianism, On Liberty and Considerations on Representative Government* (London: Everyman's Library, 1910; 1984), p. 225. In this passage from *Consideration on Representative Government* Mill goes on to talk about representation of the working class in legislatures, to which the considerations advanced here also apply. The argument does not apply, however, to representation of the working class in administrative and judicial positions, for as soon as men and women achieve the minimal qualifications necessary for such positions, they have left "the working class."

15. The day after the *New York Times* reported the Dallas Fire Department lawsuit referred to above, it reported a jury finding of discrimination by Baccarat, makers of fine glassware, against a Puerto Rican employee. This of course was not a class action lawsuit against a major corporation. But the timing is suggestive. It would be hard to find any lengthy period of time in which no such story appeared in the "newspaper of record."

16. "Set-asides" usually consist of the requirement that a certan proportion of government grants, loans, or contracts in a particular sector or region go to "minority-owned" businesses.

17. For example, the mind/body duality assumption, intelligence being only of the former, is a core part of the fetishism of testing. The ability of a great ballplayer to calculate the trajectory and distance of a batted ball in a split second, for example, is called "instinct" rather than "intelligence," al-

though there isn't the faintest theoretical reason to make this distinction. The same thing is true of Wayne Gretzky's ability to know not only where every player is on the ice at any moment but where they all will be a split second later; or Mia Hamm's similar ability on the soccer field. "Instinct for the game," or unparalleled analytical brilliance?

18. Other than teaching economics, is there *anything* one would hire Thomas Sowell to do if Jennifer Rizzotti, who undoubtedly scored lower on "objective tests," was available? Even in combat one would surely rather have her on one's team than him (or myself).

19. It's important to be clear about exactly what is happening in these circumstances. Only at institutions that make decisions based on GPAs and SATs alone is it possible to say that some students were admitted *solely* as the beneficiaries of affirmative action. Their scores, that is, were below what was otherwise defined as the "admit" level. By the same token, the candidates they replace (in the sense that the latter have a justiciable claim to have been dropped from the "admit" list in favor of affirmative action candidates) will often themselves have been at the bottom of the "admit" pile, or else they would not have been the ones replaced. This whole discussion, in other words, is often about competing applicants, *none of whom* has done especially well by the "objective test" standard of a particular institution. This is the most frequent (though not the only) circumstance in which it can plausibly be said that someone was denied admittance because of "reverse discrimination." Of course this does not make the issue of principle any less central; but in such instances it does get rid of accompanying rhetoric about the "qualified" being replaced by the "unqualified."

20. This imaginary scenario is borrowed, with grateful acknowledgement, from John Rawls's notion of "the original position" and "the veil of ignorance," as developed in *A Theory of Justice*; see chapter 1, p. 11. In the original—that is, constitution-making—position, no one participating knows anything about his or her *own* social background or interests, although everyone knows the general facts of life. Thus I know that women have less chance of following uninterrupted career paths, but I don't know whether I'm a man or a woman. Whatever conclusions I reach about how to achieve equal opportunity for women, therefore, will be reached in the light of my own realization that *I* might well be a woman myself. Consider, for example, the Founding Fathers at Philadelphia. Suppose none of them had known whether he was a debtor or creditor, a slaveholder or an independent farmer in New England, but each one knew that there were more debtors than creditors, and more independent farmers than slaveholders. Would the outcome of Constitution writing have been the same?

21. In a bizarre letter to the *New York Times* of June 1, 1998, two persistent

opponents of affirmative action, Abigail and Stephen Thernstrom, complain that at Berkeley between 1987 and 1990, "forty-two percent of the 1,398 African American students" admitted "under racial preferences," whose S.A.T. scores "averaged 300 points below those of whites and Asians," failed to graduate. One can't tell from their figures how many of all "African-American students" were beneficiaries of "racial preferences," but we do know (and the Thernstroms also know) that after the abolition of those "preferences," African-American admissions to Berkeley fell almost to zero. One reads their letter again and again, hoping that it doesn't say what it clearly does say: that every year close to 200 students who would not otherwise have been there graduated from one of the best public universities in the United States, with a degree virtually assuring their economic futures, and the Thernstroms simply don't care. With them, crocodile tears reach flood level.

22. Some Jews, for example, who once fought for admission to Gentile-only country clubs for precisely this reason ought to recognize this argument without any difficulty.

Chapter 7. Why Not Equality?

1. See George Gerbner et al, "Charting the Mainstream: Television's Contributions to Political Orientations," in Donald Lazere, ed., *American Media and Mass Culture: Left Perspectives* (Berkeley: University of California Press, 1987), pp. 441–64. American commercial television is not the only model of mass visual communication available; for a description of a system that does *not* exist solely to colonize consciousness, see my account of British television in "American Television and Consumer Democracy," *Dissent* (spring 1998), pp. 38–45.

2. From Marx's introduction to the "Contribution to the Critique of Hegel's *Philosophy of Right*." See *The Marx-Engels Reader,* p. 64.

3. A very large majority of white Americans, when asked to identify their own class membership, answer "middle class." This does not mean that they have anti–working class politics or fail to identify with issues that a historian of capitalism would consider to be working-class issues; it's more a way of distancing oneself from the poor and nonwhite.

4. Like all juggernauts, this one feeds on its own momentum. Most crucially, there is copious and persuasive evidence that at least among the rich nations the extent of "illfare" is a function of relative socioeconomic distance ("relative deprivation") rather than absolute levels of poverty. See, e.g., the data on mortality and income distribution in Richard G. Wilkinson, "Health inequalities: relative or absolute material standards?" *British Medical Jour-*

nal 314, February 22, 1997, pp. 591–94. The same is true of the spread of "illfare" across a society; e.g., epidemic illnesses, violent crime, and low birth weight are "markers of an accelerating *regional* synergism of plagues, a diffusing system of interacting and self- reinforcing pathology fueled by, but spreading far beyond, the worst affected inner-city areas." See R. Wallace, D. Wallace, and H. Andrews, "AIDS, tuberculosis, violent crime and low birthweight in eight US metropolitan areas: public policy, stochastic resonance, and the regional diffusion of inner-city markers," *Environment and Planning A*, 1997, vol. 29, p. 525 ff. The more things fall into disrepair, of course, the costlier it becomes to fix them.

5. See chapter 2, note 1. The term "authoritarian populism" was developed in the 1970s primarily by the British sociologist Stuart Hall to describe the movement toward Thatcherism. In his words, "the balance in the relation of force was moving — in that 'unstable equilibrium' between coercion and consent which characterizes *all* democratic class politics — decisively towards the 'authoritarian' pole." This movement, however, was in some degree "pioneered by, harnessed to, and to some extent legitimated by a populist groundswell below," which took "the shape of a sequence of 'moral panics,' around such apparently non-political issues as race, law-and-order, permissiveness and social anarchy." These serve "to win for the authoritarian closure the gloss of popular consent." The United States obviously is not like centralized, illiberal Great Britain; a Supreme Court justice such as Antonin Scalia, who seems to fit the authoritarian populist description in some contexts, defends flag-burning as an exercise of free speech rights. But since the first election of Richard Nixon, and George Wallace's campaign during that election, the issues identified by Hall have been at the forefront of the conservative legislative agenda. See Stuart Hall's summary, "Authoritarian Populism: A Reply to Jessop et al," *New Left Review* no. 151 (May/June 1985), p. 116.

6. Patricia Williams, *The Alchemy of Race and Rights* (Cambridge, MA.: Harvard University Press, 1991), ch. 3.

7. Antonio Gramsci, *Selections from the Prison Notebooks*, ed. and trans. by Quintin Hoare and Geoffrey Nowell Smith (New York: International Publishers, 1971), p. 275–76.

8. Compare the cautious optimism of Gunnar Myrdal's classic, *An American Dilemma* (New York: Harper & Brothers, 1944). Myrdal thought that what he deemed the dominant American liberal ideology of the Declaration of Independence and the Gettysburg Address would finally triumph over the racist practices that he saw as deviations from it. The liberal ideology remains dominant: no white comic tells racist jokes in public, and no landlord

says "Go away, nigger," when meeting a prospective renter. But housing discrimination on the basis of race remains as endemic as it ever was.

9. Rawls, for example, discusses only what in the European tradition is rather optimistically called "the law of nations." (op. cit., pp. 378–79). Michael Walzer, who differs from Rawls on many other points, also adopts the integrity of the nation-state as a principle in his *Just and Unjust Wars* (New York: Basic Books, 1977). He discusses whether "we" should have intervened in South Africa, e.g., but not whether "I" should or should not have helped run guns to the A.N.C. The only major contemporary exception is Amartya K. Sen, who, not surprisingly, writes from the standpoint of an Indian rather than European or North American economic theorist.

10. Most notable, perhaps, is Eqbal Ahmad, "The Neo-Fascist State: Notes on the Pathology of Power in the Third World," *Arab Studies Quarterly* vol. 3 no. 2 (spring 1981), 170–80. See also Vandana Shiva, *The Violence of the Green Revolution: Third World Agriculture, Ecology, and Politics* (London: Zed Books, 1991) and M. R. Bhagavan, "A Critique of India's Economic Policies and Strategies," *Monthly Review* vol. 39 no. 3 (July–August 1987), pp. 56–79; Carlos Maria Vilas, *Between Earthquakes and Volcanoes: Market, State, and the Revolutions in Central America* (New York: Monthly Review Press, 1995), or the extensive Spanish-language bibliography in Joseph Collins and John Lear, *Chile's Free-Market Miracle: A Second Look* (Oakland, Calif.: The Institute for Food and Development Policy, 1995); Larbi Sadiki, "Al-La Nidam — an Arab View of the New World (Dis)Order," *Arab Studies Quarterly* vol. 17 no. 3 (summer 1995), pp. 1–22; and Samir Amin, *Capitalism in the Age of Globalization: The Management of Contemporary Society* (London: Zed Books, 1997).

11. See, for example, Walzer's *Spheres of Justice*, pp. 28–30 (although it's doubtful if the liberal social democrat Walzer is himself a "communitarian" in the contemporary sense of that epithet); for a representative instance of postmodernist discourse, the essays (especially Butler's) in Seyla Benhabib, Judith Butler, Drucilla Cornell, and Nancy Fraser, *Feminist Contentions: A Philosophical Exchange* (New York: Routledge, 1995).

12. See J. K. Gibson-Graham, "Querying Globalization," in *Rethinking Marxism* vol. 9 no. 1, 1996–97, 1–27; 21. ("J. K. Gibson-Graham" is the pen name of Julie Graham and Katherine Gibson.) Writing from a much different perspective Ben Barber, in his *Jihad vs. McWorld* (New York: Times Books, 1995), in effect explains the resurgence of Islamic fundamentalism as a result of uneven development; and he predicts that in the end it will be defeated by the culture of "McWorld." The missing term here, as he notes himself, is democracy; and we could say alternatively that what is missing (perhaps temporarily) from this polarity, and what his analysis neglects to

consider, is any effective democratic opposition to capitalism on a global rather than merely local scale.

13. This argument does not necessarily vitiate Walzer's notion of "shared understandings," since he might agree (my reading of *Spheres of Justice* is that he does agree) that in this particular case *every* cultural tradition holds certain kinds of economic domination or monopoly to be wrong.

14. John Stuart Mill, *The Subjection of Women* (Arlington Heights, Ill.: Harlan Davidson, 1980), p. 56. Although we owe this perfected logical point to Mill, he is otherwise in fact less free of traditional attitudes about women than Wollstonecraft.

15. On the role of gender in the globalized political economy see Enloe's "The Globetrotting Sneaker," *Ms.*, vol. 5 no. 5 (March/April 1995), pp. 10–15.

16. See Manning Marable, *How Capitalism Underdeveloped Black America: Problems in Race, Political Economy, and Society* (Boston: South End Press, 1983).

17. See, for example, Michael Walzer's discussion of the Italo-American sanitation workers of San Francisco, the "San Francisco Scavengers," in *Spheres of Justice*, op. cit., pp. 177–183.

Chapter 8. Conclusion: Egalitarian Solidarity

1. Roosevelt's words are emblazoned on one of the walls of the FDR Memorial in Washington, D.C. Bay's remark, from *The Structure of Freedom*, is the culmination of an argument that begins on p. 3 of that book and climaxes on p. 7.

2. Again, Swedish egalitarianism had the limits of coexisting with a capitalist economic structure. Collective bargaining could not narrow the *wealth* gap between Swedish workers — well or poorly paid — and Swedish industrialists.

3. Of course there was no "general strike" in the United States in that period, but there were various municipal general strikes (Seattle, Tacoma, Minneapolis, San Francisco) that led up to the great occupations and sitdowns at the major auto works. These in turn resonated throughout the nation, so that, for example, the women of Woolworth's department stores joined the men of Flint Number One in "sitting down." The National Labor Relations Act of 1937 was framed and debated in direct response to this movement. See Jeremy Brecher, *Strike!* (Boston: South End Press, 1972). For the more common experience of labor action, see Rick Fantasia, *Cultures of Solidarity: Consciousness, Action, and Contemporary American Workers* (Berkeley: University of California Press, 1988). The ordinary strike is real and inspiring, and often culturally transformative. But politically it is evanescent. As

to why this is so, the best account is probably Mike Davis's *Prisoners of the American Dream: Politics and Economy in the History of the U.S. Working Class* (London: Verso Books, 1986); and Gary Gerstle's *Working-Class Americanism: The Politics of Labor in a Textile City, 1914–1960* (New York: Cambridge University Press, 1989). These studies describe the difficulty of mobilizing Americans en masse but do not question the necessity of it.

4. See Milner, op. cit., for his discussion of the "wage solidarity policy."

5. In order to avoid confusion, it's important to stipulate that majority rule is *necessary* but *not sufficient* for political equality. Minority right is also necessary (but not sufficient). Minority rule, unlike majority rule, is neither necessary nor sufficient for political equality. A federation of associated polities, each armed with a discretionary veto power, might in some cases seem to be a preferable alternative to a unitary state. However, this alternative does not dispense with majority rule but merely relocates it to within each of the associated polities. Moreover, I would strongly dispute whether any federation could exist for long if the federated peoples felt only internal solidarity with each other and none toward those others with whom they were "federated." This would be the United Nations, or the European Economic Union, as polities: and as now constituted they aren't polities, egalitarian or otherwise.

6. See, for example, Iris Marion Young's *Justice and the Politics of Difference* (Princeton: Princeton University Press, 1990), especially chapters 2 and 5.

7. Gitlin, *The Twilight of Common Dreams: Why America Is Wracked by Culture Wars* (New York: Henry Holt and Company, 1995).

8. Liberal constitutionalism is not the *only* American ideology. But it is overwhelmingly dominant, as can be seen in the way it is paid homage by its *soi-disant* enemies. When D'nesh D'Souza, e.g., decries the alleged triumphs of "illiberal education," he is invoking what he savages from the other side of his mouth. The word "liberal" has the same historical etymology in the two apparently disparate contexts. In each case, especially, institutional neutrality among competing values is a *sine qua non*. The attack on "political correctness" is a demand that institutions of higher education "return" to that alleged state of political neutrality (they never practiced it, in fact). In the same way, the development of "race" as a protected category is a direct development from Harlan's ideal of "color blindness."

9. This remains true even as the Rehnquist Court leads a retreat from affirmative action. Its retreat is a lot more orderly and slightly more nuanced than that mandated by, for example, the people and governor of California.

10. In my hearing a prominent leader of the New Democratic Party of Canada once referred to feminist demands on that party as "destructive" and "obscene." At that moment one could confidently have removed the NDP from

the roster of candidates for the future leadership of Canadian egalitarianism.

11. It might seem odd to speak of freedom from fear of crime as a "privilege." But that's exactly what it is. What whites who move to suburbs or call for more toughness on crime want is precisely to be free of the threat that ghettoized urban black people live with because the same concatenation of private and public lending and building practices that created the white suburbs also forced blacks into urban ghettos.

12. Jodi Dean, *Solidarity of Strangers: Feminism after Identity Politics* (Berkeley: University of California Press, 1996), p. 178. See also the discussion of inclusion and exclusion by bell hooks, *Feminist Theory: From Margin to Center* (Boston: South End Press, 1984), pp. 43–65.

13. This is the whining litany of D'Souza and similar opponents of "political correctness," who are actually themselves about as faithful supporters of liberal tolerance as the average slaveholder was. D'Souza came to fame as part of a movement of viciously bigoted Dartmouth students who among their other "politically incorrect" behaviors actually set out deliberately to destroy the career of a black member of the music department, publicly using the vilest racist (and other) slurs imaginable to drive him from the classroom. Next, I suppose, David Duke will be complaining about the illiberal treatment of Nazis.

14. This is not meant as a judgment in principle. There are certainly coherent and intelligent defenses of the idea of putting more emphasis on local dialects or languages than is currently the case in American public education; the politics of the Oakland debate made it less than that, however.

15. Public discussion on the question of universals versus relativism is often confused by the fact that it's quite possible, indeed frequent, for a person to argue correctly on behalf of universally valid standards and yet be quite wrongheaded about what they are in particular. This is an argument not against the existence of universal moral truths but against such a person's politics, morality, or philosophy.

16. For an articulation of the principle of solidarity from the outside looking in, see Bernice Johnson Reagon, "Coalition Politics: Turning the Century," in Barbara Smith, ed., *Homegirls: A Black Feminist Anthology* (New York: Kitchen Table—Women of Color Press, 1983). A black woman addressing an audience of mostly white women at a women's music festival, Reagon (a member of the singing group Sweet Honey in the Rock) says, "That is often what it feels like if you're *really* doing coalition work. Most of the time you feel threatened to the core and if you don't, you're not really doing no coalescing" (p. 356). The principle of mutual recognition has serious costs for

everyone; it is the ineluctability of these costs that Gitlin, for one, fails to grasp.

17. The discussion from p. 188 forward benefitted greatly from the suggestions of Gina Rourke and Robert Paul Wolff.

18. Understanding the difference, we see how supposedly troubling institutions such as nonconsensual female genital "circumcision" are actually non-issues. Far from being a defense of a human right by an oppressed people for whom it is culturally a human right, it is actually an attack on the human rights of some of those people. It doesn't matter what "culture" one lives in; "no" always means "no."

19. Conversely, the children of secularists are not unfairly deprived of anything by not being taught "creation science," because there is no such thing.

INDEX